Your child needs music!

Barbara Cass-Beggs

Your Child
Needs Music

Dedication

This book is written for and dedicated to those who are concerned about music in early childhood education.

My thanks go to David (my husband) for his understanding help, Michael (my son) for helping to edit this book — and Evy Pareskevopoulos with whom I have worked for many years and who continues to be a source of inspiration.

* * *

Know you what it is to be a child? It is to be something very different from the man of today. It is to have a spirit yet streaming from the waters of baptism; it is to believe in love, to believe in loveliness, to believe in belief; it is to be so little that the elves can reach to whisper in your ear; it is to turn pumpkins into coaches, and mice into horses, lowness into loftiness, and nothing into everything, for each child has a fairy godmother in his own soul; it is to live in a nutshell and count yourself the king of infinite space..."

— Francis Thompson-Shelley

Foreword

I had the honour and pleasure to take part in the work of Mrs. Barbara Cass-Beggs with babies and children. The first time was in 1983, when I was invited to demonstrate my method "Children Paint Music" in Ottawa at the "Listen, Like, Learn" music conference. The second time was when she came to Vienna at the invitation of the Ministry of Art and Education and gave some lectures. In Barbara Cass-Beggs' methods I found all the prerequisites that I consider important for a truly good music lesson: opening the ear for sounds, noises, and melodies; the involvement of the mother; awakening a feeling of rhythm, and getting acquainted with different kinds of music and instruments.

As far as my experience with Mrs. Cass-Beggs' pupils is concerned, I have held innumerable courses with my method "Children Paint Music" over the last ten years. Some 1,500 children have listened to music with me from Vienna to New York, and from Malta to Ottawa. Both older children and the very young, like those in Canada, have studied with me. But no where else have I found such ears as I did among the children in Barbara Cass-Beggs' school.

Klara Kern
Professor of Music
Vienna, Austria

Introduction

Over a period of several years I have been privileged to be associated with Barbara Cass-Beggs in her work with children and music. It is regrettable that the printed page can communicate only a small portion of Barbara's method. Those of us who have had the opportunity to watch her with children in a musical experience more fully appreciate the dynamic which results when Barbara, children and music converge in a dynamic experience. As a music teacher, Barbara has clearly set her priorities on children and is cognisant of the effect of a total environment on children and consequently she involves them in all aspects of musical experience. It is a particular treat to watch her communicate through music with infants well before they are able to utter their first words.

As an educator with sparse musical background I have been intrigued to interpret and analyze Barbara's methods in terms of pedagogical theory. Her approach is facilitative rather than intrusive since she respects the integrity of each child as a unique and worthy person. This respect for uniqueness extends as well to her colleagues. As a leader in this field Barbara demonstrates that to be successful, other music teachers may follow her lead but to be fully effective, they should avoid rote copying of her programmes. Indeed, she encourages her colleagues to pursue the development of their own methods and approaches, incorporating the best and most appropriate influences from Barbara's and others' techniques which they have experienced.

I would hope and expect that this book should be such an influence on the styles of parents and teachers who read it.

William Bélanger
Dept. of Education, University of Ottawa

Preface

My aim in this book is to draw attention to some of the tested methods, and suggest that through the **Listen, Like, Learn** approach, parents and teachers may find additional ways of interesting young children in music.

It is now some time since my book *To Listen, To Like, To Learn* (now out of print), was published. Further experience has shown that my fundamental principles still work, so I restate them here. There are, additionally, a sufficient number of new ideas and necessary revisions to make this new book worth while.

For many years now I have been introducing babies, with their mothers and/or fathers, to music, through my more recent book *Your Baby Needs Music*. As this is a new educational concept, a majority of parents and teachers are unaware of the musical possibilities at babyhood and I therefore include a chapter on introducing your baby to music.

Because music needs to be regarded as an integral part of a child's life, and related to the other arts such as poetry, dance, drama and painting, I include here a chapter on the Arts and how to include them in a music programme.

All parents and teachers need to know how children learn, and what makes learning easy and efficient, so this is discussed in chapter one. Attention is also drawn to the importance of physical movement (chapter five), which is inevitably bound up with music, since all music is movement.

Naturally, singing is emphasized, for every child has a voice, and this is the child's natural instrument.

In discovering the musical aspects of dynamics and form, the value and use of instruments, particularly the simple percussion instruments, is examined.

Special attention is paid to making *reading music* both easy and enjoyable, as reading is a skill which is often neglected.

Finally, whatever aspects of music are discussed, I stress 'listening to music", for music is a listening subject.

Because two groups of people who are not necessarily trained musicians are inevitably involved in music-making with young children or babies, this book is addressed to these parents and school teachers, and although the material is directed to the young child of two to six and covers a three-year learning period, it is suitable for any age of musical "beginner" and any experience level of teacher or parent. Teachers always hope that one day they will find one perfect musical method which will cover all their musical contingencies. Alas! There is no such one infallible method, and good teachers soon learn to pick and choose, suiting their musical approach to the type of children that they are teaching and their material to the country in which they happen to live.

As singing is so important, it is necessary to familiarize ourselves with songs which are simple and musically satisfying and at the same time relate to the child. Luckily, *nursery rhymes* and *folk songs* can supply us with exactly this type of song, and as every country has grown its own folk music, there is an inexhaustible supply of good and appropriate material. Such good songs have an added advantage from the point of view of pitch and key, for they are usually well within the range of the young child's voice, (an octave or eight notes) and they are often modal, so that the child is not limited to major and minor keys. In addition, these songs and rhymes are usually made up by ordinary people, not musicians as such, and are concerned with everyday happenings, which children appreciate. They also provide a social history of the country to which they belong. Canadian folk songs, having grown out of two cultures: French and English, can help children acquire a working knowledge of the two languages. (In Canada we owe much to the folk song collections of Marius Barbeau, Helen Creighton, Edith Fowke, Louise Manny, Kenneth Peacock and many others.)

Because parents and teachers can now purchase a number of excellent song books and books containing music to movement, I have only included songs and music which are directly related to what I am talking about, or are not easily available. There are also a few well-known songs that I mention which I do not feel it necessary to include. As I feel that the majority of songs for young children should be sung *unaccompanied*, I have only added a few accompaniments, but I have put in guitar chording, which can, of course, assist the pianist or anyone playing the autoharp.

Naturally, the aim of this book and the aim of all those who are trying to extend the musical boundaries for children, can only be accomplished if music, and the arts in general, are not only readily available but are treated with the respect that they deserve. Sad to say, this is not generally the case. The arts are rarely given first priority and are usually the first subjects to be cut when educational authorities or governments need to save money. Therefore, it is important that we, as musicians and teachers, who are concerned with music, should be able to present convincing reasons why there should be *more* not *less* attention given to music and the arts, both in our schools and in our homes, for it is particularly important for the young child to be able to experience music." In my work as director of the University of Toronto Settlement Music School, I was often asked why it was considered necesary to bring music to the underprivileged children of that neighbour-hood. Wasn't it enough to help them with food and clothing? Certainly, I agreed, these were the basic things, but there are other essentials. There is an old Chinese proverb which says "if you have two loaves, sell one and buy a lily," for wise people realize the lily is more essential to real living than the second loaf.

Music can bring a sense of pride and worth to the dispossessed. It can break down barriers of race, culture and language; for in a variety of forms music is common to all races and cultures, and enjoyment of music can transcend these differences.

In our leisure time we all need relaxing and stimulating things to do and if we don't get them in one way we will get them in another. Street gangs? or participation in a choir or band? The violence of a poor television programme? or the pleasure and stimulation of watching an exciting play or ballet? The dullness of "spectator" events, which often need to be enlivened by drugs or drink? or the mental and physical challenge of learning to play an instrument, and winning the undivided attention of one listener? It usually depends not so much on *choice* but on what is available at the moment, and what is available *when* it is needed.

One of our very talented girls in the Settlement ballet group phoned one day to say that her family had been evicted and would I please come and rescue the piano. When I got there everything they possessed was out in the street. When I asked if there was anything else of importance, she said "No, I have the other important things here," and showed me her ballet shoes and tunic which were hidden under her coat.

In initiating junior concerts for the younger children in the schools of Saskatchewan I found that these were often the child's first contact with "live" music. At first some of the schools thought that children would never enjoy "concerts" but the demand has continued to grow and these concerts have become part of the life of the province. And why? Because having been introduced to live music, the children found it stimulating and enjoyable and wanted to explore it further in their leisure time. Naturally, the idea of a "concert" worried many of them to begin with, but once we got them to *one* concert the rest was easy, and as one of my more reluctant attenders remarked, "Well, if that's a concert, I like 'em!"

People are only too ready to think that children will not enjoy "the best" which is certainly not the case, and they are also only too ready to measure education in terms of dollars and cents and so-called "practicality". When children joined our Settlement music school we were fairly certain that by degrees, what they did with us, would prove more interesting than smashing cars, or getting hooked on drugs or drink. So *more* support for arts and music and good leisure-time programmes would actually save money spent fixing vandalism and stopping crime, let alone children's lives!

Musical and artistic needs are of paramount importance, for it is the heart and not the head which actually guides our life and destiny, and, in understanding the emotional needs of people we can plan a secure future for mankind. It is to be hoped that parents, educators and governments will discover, before it is too late, that the truly practical subjects are those which deal not only with the intellect but with the emotions, too. Much has been written on this subject and further information can be found in the articles and books listed in the Bibliography.

In closing, I cannot resist quoting from H.S. Broudy: "Aesthetic experience is basic, because it is the primary form of experience on which all cognitive judgment and action depend. It is the fundamental and distinctive power of image-making by the imagination, and it furnishes the raw material for concepts and ideals for creating a world of possibilities."

— *Barbara Cass-Beggs*, April, 1985, Ottawa, Canada

⁕ See Chapter on **Reading Music: Melody, Pitch & Solfége.**
⁕⁕ **We would not even be in the position that we are now, were it not for the work of those musical pioneers who had taken a special interest in music as related to the young child. Kodály, Orff, Dalcroze, Curwen and Suzuki. (See Appendix VIII).**

Table of Contents

Music and your child's learning process

Your child must *like* music before he/she can *learn* it. The earlier she learns to listen to music and enjoy it, the more she is likely to benefit. You should know, however, what learning conditions need to be discovered by observing your child's responses, or better still, the responses of the baby, who cannot be *persuaded* to respond. Once you have discovered what these conditions are, compare them with the method and philosophy of your present teaching method to determine what changes would be helpful.

Here are some conditions which may help your child to learn music more effectively:

- **Security and Stability:** Uncertainty and confusion are obviously detrimental to your child's peace of mind and ability to learn. Therefore, to make your child feel secure you need to have a musical outline, and your schedule, which should follow a logical sequence, should be selected according to your child's ability to learn within certain time limits.

- **Curiosity:** The next step is to discover how to arouse your child's curiosity. Children learn *because* they are curious. A child has the ability to feel, taste, smell, look, and hear. She is curious about all aspects of herself, and all are systematically explored. These explorations and their results, providing no one inhibits her, serve to further arouse her curiosity.

- **Feelings and Emotions:** These are an integral part of her development as they provide the power that triggers interest in new things. Babies are especially dependent on feelings and emotions in order to learn, for in the early years these take precedence over the cognitive and intellectual skills. The use of imaginative and emotional skills is still a vital learning tool, although its effect on a child's later development is often underestimated.

- **Imitation:** The active enjoyment of imitation plays a major role in the learning process. If your child can satisfy her curiosity, feelings, emotions and imitate those she loves there is no reason why she shouldn't learn all the time! Isn't it the adult, not the child, who thinks learning is something unnatural, difficult, or boring?

- **Variety:** Babies love novelty, not tedium. They enjoy complex patterns and bright colours, and dislike over-repetitiveness and lack of imagination. Because of their short attention span, babies and young children concentrate better when they are not expected to participate in one event for very long.

Fear and anxiety are detrimental to learning, for both block the biological plan for learning and are the worst enemies of intelligence. If your child is fearful or anxious, not only does she lose the desire to learn, but is physically unable to learn effectively. All children need to feel secure and unafraid before they can give their full attention to learning.

Fear, however, should not be confused with stress, for stress, to a certain degree, can have a very positive effect on your child's ability to learn. During the learning process your child moves into the unknown and unpredictable (stress) and then back to the known and predictable (relaxation). This stress-relaxation rhythm is an ability which should be encouraged and developed. Physical strength grows through the stressing and relaxing of the muscles; a developed intelligence grows through the successful practice of the stress-relaxation principle.

In challenging your child, try to avoid boredom, but at the same time see see that she is not overwhelmed. Perhaps, by two personal experiences, I can illustrate what I mean:

A five-year-old, who counted well and knew what numbers were, came home from kindergarten one day saying she "hated numbers."

"Why?" we asked.

"Oh," she said, "It makes my hand so tired colouring twelve monkeys."!

At the end of a music class when an unusual amount of new material had been presented, one of the brightest of the six-year-olds sighed, and said, "Well, it's been nice, but you have given me too *much* music today."

All young children need movement. So in order to learn effectively, movement and the value of *doing,* hearing, and seeing cannot be over-estimated. These ingredients need to be part of every music session. When your child hears, sees, and makes music, it becomes part of her. The physically handicapped child often becomes the mentally handicapped child simply because, as a baby, she has been unable to repeat the many intricate movements and sounds which are necessary to develop both her physical and mental capabilities.

Because young children use all the avenues of their senses simultaneously to understand the world in which they live, music makes more sense if it is treated as part of their lives, rather than an isolated experience. Music therefore is more effective if it can relate closely to the other arts, such as dance, drama, poetry and painting. A song can be danced, dramatized, painted, with each aspect adding something to its value and interest. In this way, music can be enhanced through the movement of a dance or the dramatic interpretation of a mood.[1]

A distinguishing feature that makes mankind unique is the need to communicate, and through communication, to socialize. Babies coo, babble, and sing before they speak. So singing *to* and *with* your child, increases her enjoyment of sound and her understanding of speech, which is basic to the whole learning process. Because the human voice is the most natural instrument, and since singing is a spontaneous action, singing provides the first, and continually important, means of musical expression. Singing together gives a sense of security, and the secure child is the receptive child.

With today's emphasis on the "ready made," a minor but helpful condition for learning is to encourage parents and teachers to make more musical items themselves.[2]

In early paintings, such as those by Breughel, children are shown dressed exactly like adults. Now, clothes are designed specifically to suit children and to allow them to develop more naturally. Evidence suggests that

[1] See Chapter 10 "How and Why the Arts relate to Music"
[2] See Chapter 6.

the child's brain needs its own natural approach to learning through play and involvement in the arts and this is borne out in a number of recent studies on the human brain.

Although there is insufficient agreement on such studies as a proven educational approach, they are still worth considering. The main thesis states that a child's brain develops through a non-verbal or intuitive method of communication. Research indicates that children need to approach learning through the development of avenues of sensory perception. Such an approach lays a firm foundation for abstract and analytical reasoning and the decoding of symbols which follows when the child is intellectually ready.[3]

The most rapid learning takes place during the first three or four years of a child's life; although there is no time limit to the ability to learn. Experience gained in enrichment programs also show that it is more difficult for a child to catch up if she has been frustrated or retarded in her early years. These statements confirm what was said earlier: in order for your child to learn effectively, the teaching of music should start as soon as possible when the child is at her peak of curiosity..

Let's take a closer look at some of our learning conditions.

It is important that you take a critical look at the musical outlines or "syllabuses" that are available. Many need bringing up to date; some follow too slavishly one school of thought and, as a result, may not satisfy all your needs; others have a too elaborate and rigid program which leaves no time or space for the teacher's or child's creative thinking. When you select musical material for the classroom or home, keep in mind the culture of the country and the type of children you are teaching. Planning is necessary but there must be room for spontaneity and adaptation which are part of the creative process of teaching. It is only too easy, in a search for security, to establish "cults" which in time lead to rigidity.

Repetition to a certain extent is both necessary and enjoyable. A method based on repetition and memory, however, is inadequate unless you accompany this with a better understanding of music and progress in the child's ability to read music.

The stress-relaxation principle is always involved in the challenge of learning something new. However the tense child who is unable to relax even when she has accomplished what she wanted to do, may need to learn how to relax by moving or by listening to reposeful and relaxed music.

Movement is valuable in order to express the hearing and seeing aspect of music. This can be helped by the use of the Curwen-Solfége and hand signs, and also by the countless variations of movement to music. You should never forget, however, that listening is the most essential part of all music training. Generally speaking, there is a great deal of stress on seeing, rather than hearing in a child's education and when the listening aspect is neglected, children may develop speech defects or have a difficult time reading fluently.

---

[3]
English, W., *Brian Research and Music* (paper presented at the C.M.E.A., Vancouver, B'C" 1979), and Wilson. D., *Implications of Brain Learning* (paper presented at the I.S.M.E., Poland, 1980).

Keeping curiosity alive is no problem for there is always something new in music to discover and explore. Music also provides a natural vehicle for the expression of emotional and imaginative skills.

Children aren't usually afraid in a music class unless they feel that too much is expected of them. Fear can develop if they are confused, or if they have to play or move despite their fears. With care, music can play an important part in alleviating fears. Singing, conducting, clapping a rhythm, playing a percussion instrument successfully are all important sources in building up a child's confidence. A key condition for learning is enjoyment and enjoyment is expressed in a variety of different ways, for every child enjoys different things at different times.

There is the enjoyment which comes from the security of repeating what is known and loved, of being challenged by something new and difficult, of being "entertained," and there is the pleasure of group participation. Perhaps the most rewarding of all is the enjoyment of listening to music itself. With any luck — if we have done our job adequately (discover how the child learns and how we can best help her enjoy learning) this enjoyment of music will remain with her for the rest of her life.

In reading this book, I hope you will return to this chapter from time to time and use it as a "touchstone". I am sure you will also want to list your own methods for predisposing your child to learn music effectively.

The Listen, Like, Learn Approach

My approach has grown out of the kind of musical experience I have found children respond well to: *Listening,* because he enjoys music; *liking,* because he is participating; and *learning,* which is wanting to discover something more about music.

As all successful teaching involves practical planning as well as philosophy, here is an outline of some of the steps which need to be taken before embarking on the *Listen, Like, Learn* approach.

1. The basic aim of this course is to help children listen to music. Therefore, in addition to the actual class music, information about "what is going to happen next" is expressed musically. (see Information Music)

2. Because young children like a sense of order and security, music class activities should occur in a certain sequence. For example: open with the same song, "See My Fingers," and close with the same song, "Off We Go On Our Ponies," or "Candle Burning Bright."

3. Because young children are very active, a spacious, carpeted or not slippery, area will be required. Children must take off their shoes, and preferably their socks, so their feet can feel the music.

4. In a private class, I have found that ten children form an ideal number. In such instances, I consider it necessary to have one teaching assistant. They are needed to help in emergencies and generally to keep things running smoothly. In a school, nursery school, or day care centre, where many more children participate, there may not be additional teachers to help. This type of program, however, is even more valuable than the private music class because it reaches a greater number of children.

5. Parents are useful helpers. Difficulties, though, can arise if they are involved with their own child. In the private class, I like to invite one parent a time to take a turn at being present, and all of them to be present at the final class (which I do not regard as a performance, but just another class).

6. Each child should have a workbook, (a large scrapbook) which is used each week. These books help the parents to see what their child is doing. Everyone, staff and children alike, make better progress when the parents are kept constantly informed. When holding a private class, I invite parents to come to an "initiation" meeting where we discuss and illustrate what their children will learn and how we go about the whole process. This type of meeting should also be offered in a school, nursery school, or daycare setting.

7. Because there are so many exciting and different things to do, I find that in the private music class an hour's program is about the right length. With two-year-olds, however, we break in the middle of the program for juice and cookies. In school, nursery school, or the day care centre it is probably better to have a shorter music session, say twenty to thirty minutes, but every day, if possible!

8. By the time the children are five and a half, or six*, they should be reading music fairly easily. At this stage I invite artists, friends, parents, or students, to come and play to them, to introduce the different musical Families: Woodwind, Brass, and Percussion. Parents are invited to attend. At these sessions children not only listen to the instruments, but are allowed to try them. Then they are asked to consider which instrument they would like to learn (keep in mind that not every child wants to play an instrument).

Musical Information

* The program outlined in this book covers about three years, so children starting at six would be 8 or 9 at this stage.

Books a-way books a-way Put your books a-way to day.

With today's small-sized instruments it is not difficult to choose one they are capable of playing. Having kept in touch with some of my pupils for many years, I find that although they may learn an additional instrument, they usually keep to the one they originally chose for themselves.

9. Regarding equipment, one needs an: Orff tambour, rhythm sticks, (two for each child), bells, rattles, and the usual percussion instruments (see Chapter 6, Percussion). It is nice to have a piano but a guitar or autoharp can be a good substitute. If the teacher plays another instrument, such as a cello or violin, these too can be used to advantage. A "Music Corner", where a variety of home-made and percussion instruments is available, is essential for every nursery school, or day care centre.

10. Children need to *see* music in order to realize that it is a "written" as well as a "listened to" language. Easy melodies and rhythms can be hung on walls. Nursery rhyme picture books with music might also be made available.

Music is an important and enjoyable subject. Although we do not expect children participating in music classes to necessarily become professional musicians, they can *all* become better, more mature human beings or, in future, a discriminating audience. Whether we teach music as part of a school, nursery school, or daycare program, or in special classes on a private basis, the aim is the same — to expose children to music so that they can have the opportunity of enjoying it and accepting it as part of their lives. They will then probably grow up enjoying music and will want to continue to listen to music throughout their lives.

OFF WE GO
Folk Flemish

Off we go on our po- nies, our po- nies, our po- nies. Off we go on our po- nies whoa, whoa, whoa.

Verse 2   Gallop and gallop and gallop etc...

SEE MY FINGERS

See my fin—gers dance and play, fin—gers dance for me to day.
See my ten toes dance and play, ten toes dance for me to day.

CANDLE BURNING BRIGHT

Can-dle burn-ing bright glis-tening in the night.

We must say good bye to you and blow the can-dle out.

Each child is "blown out" in turn and runs away to get dressed

Lesson planning

Although it is not possible or desirable to give detailed lesson plans (for every teacher needs to plan her own work) some suggestions on how to use the material in chapters four to eleven, and what one can expect to accomplish in first and subsequent years, seem appropriate.

Certainly music classes must be enjoyable; however, in order to continue to be enjoyable, there must be progress, challenge and some effort on the part of the children, for children do not really enjoy "messing about" or "attending a program" which goes nowhere. Children like to feel that they are accomplishing something, and being taken seriously.

Personally, although I have taught for many years I still plan each lesson, write it out, and check at the end of the class to see what I have left out or what new item went particularly well. A good music class, to an outsider, can look like a "spontaneous happening" but I would agree with Harry Belafonte who said, when asked about the spontaneity of his programs, "If you only knew how many hours of work go into looking spontaneous!"

In the children's first year of music classes, which in many ways is the most important year, time should be spent discovering what music is about, getting to know the children, discovering their possibilities, and concentrating on "experience" not "facts".

The basic elements of the *Listen - Like - Learn* program are the basic elements of music, which are: singing, movement, rhythm and melody, and these elements can only be introduced successfully if, at the same time, the children are learning to listen.

The introduction of percussion and melodic instruments is important because these can be used to accompany songs, enliven and assist rhythmic and melodic work and contribute to dynamics, expression and form.

Musical enrichment, which is discussed in terms of dynamics, expression and form, is not treated so much as a subject on its own, but as something which impinges on every aspect of music. Naturally the Arts, in the forms of painting, drama and dance add still further to the enrichment of almost any aspect of our music classes. Perhaps if we look at the musical aspects that we have been discussing here, we might now work out what we can expect our children to know at the end of one year, and subsequent years. This will depend, naturally, on how many classes the children attend.

Year One

SINGING: (Chapter 4) Each class would include the opening and closing songs, three or four more songs, a singing game and always a lullaby (for lullabies are relaxing and children need to be sung to). By the end of the first year children will have listened to and participated in between thirty and forty songs (these songs are very short). They will have learned so that they can sing on their own, about ten songs. (It is important for children to hear and participate in many more songs than they will be able to learn and reproduce accurately.)

MOVEMENT (Chapter 5) There are many different ways of using movement, but in the first year one should concentrate on big, simple movements which encourage relaxation and freedom, and then move on to exercises which help the child's co-ordination. (These suggestions come at the beginning of this chapter).

INTRODUCTION OF INSTRUMENTS (Chapter 6) Almost everything in this chapter, except certain items mentioned in the children's third year, can be covered in the first year (noting that one does not use cymbals). Most of these items will be repeated in the second and third years but with the use of different music and with greater accuracy.

READING MUSIC — RHYTHM (Chapter 7) Stages one and two will probably be covered in the first year, but not necessarily, as stage one requires a lot of repetition, particularly for the two-year-olds.

READING MUSIC — MELODY (Chapter 8) Most children find the melodic approach somewhat harder to grasp than its corresponding rhythmic approach, so although you may cover stage one, you may not get more than halfway through stage two. (You will certainly want to use some of the chime bar games in stage two).

MUSICAL ENRICHMENT (Chapter 10) In this section where all the learning situations can be part of what you do in songs, movement, reading or the Arts, there are certain items which should definitely come into this first year. *Loud* and *soft, quick* and *slow, legato* and *staccato, crescendo* and *diminuendo,* and most important of all, the *sound sessions* which come at the beginning of the chapter, when the children can meet the kitchen instruments, the bells, drums, rattles, gongs and the simple percussion instruments, plus sounds which the children can find and make for themselves. Conducting can start at this time plus some exciting "listening music" sessions.

THE ARTS (Chapter II) Here, one's choice would be short poems which relate to your .subject matter, musical stories which can be dramatized through movement or percussion, song — dances such as "As I was walking down the street" and drawing or painting which can be part of any of the children's musical experiences.

Year Two

The lessons for year two would include stage three of Rhythm and Melody in Reading Music (chapters 7 & 8) and the items in chapters 4-11 which have not been covered, apart from the following items which should not be included until the third year.

Year Three

SINGING (Chapter 4) Rounds and songs with descants or alto parts. Making up songs adding ostinatos, and easy chord accompaniments.
MOVEMENT (Chapter 5) Mime and mood interpretations.
INSTRUMENTS (Chapter 6) Time recognition, formal conducting, score reading.
READING MUSIC (Chapter 9) Stage four.
ENRICHMENT (Chapter 10) Musical form, cadences, major and minor keys. One would include meeting the different musical families and choosing what instrument the children want to play. Short piano and recorder lessons could now be included in the regular class time.
THE ARTS (Chapter 11) Here we should include more set dances, some of the longer narrative poems, building a program around the life of a composer, listening to music through painting and getting a musician to come and talk and play to the class.

    Of course, what is accomplished in these three years or more is only a beginning; but we can be sure that if the children have enjoyed the beginning they will continue to enjoy and *demand* more music and play leading parts in their school's music activities.

    Year one of this syllabus should cover two and three-year-olds; year two, four and five-year-olds. If children of 8 or 9 are attending music classes for the first time, one would move quickly through the first and second year's work (which they would still need to know) and spend longer on the material in year three. However, as children's musical ability is varied and does not necessarily correspond to their chronological age, you will find that these age

1. Year Two involves a good deal of repetition, but with the expectation of a higher degree of accuracy.

groups overlap considerably. If a group of two-year-olds have had no previous experience it might be wise to use the material in the last chapter of the book *Your Baby Needs Music* before they fully participate in the first year program.

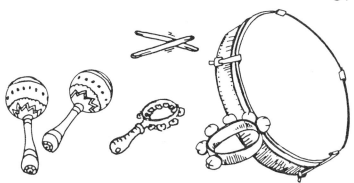

CHAPTER 3

Your baby needs music

The basic principles of the *Listen, Like, Learn* approach applies also to babies. The organization, planning and content of mother and baby groups, however, is so different that I can make no attempt to cover it here and would need to refer you to my book *Your Baby Needs Music*.

Having organized and led mother and baby (3-23 months) music groups for a long time, I am convinced that a baby's music program should be taken seriously. It should, if possible, preface any type of music program which is directed towards young children. A chapter on music for the baby, therefore, belongs in all music books concerned with the development of the whole child.

It is still too soon to say whether this early start produces more professional musicians, although I would guess that it does. It is *not* too early to demonstrate how babies and mothers who participate in a music program grow to love music, and what excellent musical progress the babies make when, at age two, they move into music classes.

Mothers, musicians, and the general public still need to be persuaded to take the subject of babies and music seriously, although mothers who have participated in these programs are completely convinced this is necessary. This lack of interest is not altogether surprising, however, when we see how little attention is given to the baby in books dealing with music and the young child, (with one exception, a book called *Music: a Way of Life for the Young Child* by Bayless and Ramsey).

Because there is a general lack of information about the effect of music on the baby, I have drawn attention to research already accomplished in this field in the hopes that this research will help to answer the type of questions so often asked, such as, "Why is a baby interested in music?" "What can music contribute to a baby's life?, or "At what stage in a baby's growth does he/she respond to sound and rhythm?"

Why Music is Important for your Baby

Based on carefully recorded observation, there has been a dramatic increase in infant research[1] since the 1950s, and, in particular, since 1975. This research has led to increased awareness of the infant's perceptual life, (mind, and senses), especially in the visual and (hitherto) less-explored auditory aspects.[2]

We have known for some time that an infant's primary needs are love and emotional security. Satisfaction of physical needs alone is not enough. It has been shown that the infant stands a better chance of developing if her environment is rich in variety, freedom, and sensory stimulation.

The experience of musicians working with babies and young children supports these findings. It is now possible to demonstrate that music can be the easiest and probably the most effective way of providing this type of enriched environment. Infants, for example, are not only aware of music, but respond to it with enjoyment. Music stimulates spontaneous motor movement, which is an essential step towards the attainment of the infant's sensory development and control; for each physical activity relates to a different part of the brain. (A five-day-old infant can turn its head to the left or right to discover the source of a sound.)

It is not surprising that the infant is aware of music; when one considers that the fetus has been conditioned to rhythm and sound since conception, and has evolved its own rhythmic movements, while in the womb.[3-4-5]

A number of research projects have been undertaken which relate to the response of the fetus to sound and the sensitivity of the neonate's hearing. Experiments have shown that the fetus reacts to sound by the twenty-ninth week before birth;[6] and that continuing the rhythm of the heartbeat after birth increases the infant's sense of security and well being.

Because the structures for hearing are well in place before birth, a baby is born with an acute sense of hearing. As she can recognize speech variation, including music, just as she is encouraged, at this time, to use her muscles. Dr. John Brierly has suggested that an infant needs meaningful sound (speech) in order to develop her own sound patterns. Even though a child is born with what amounts to a preprogrammed ability for language, this ability needs to be triggered and cultivated.[7]

Just as the fetus calms down when the mother talks quietly to it, and is lulled to sleep when she walks around, so too the infant's sense of security is helped by a mother who continues to talk to her. Croons, which are spontaneous sounds like "there, there" or "bye bye" or simple lullabies, are even more important since they are nearly always accompanied by a rocking movement which provides the necessary source of rhythmic continuity as well as speech patterning. As an infant prefers her mother's voice; therefore, it is obvious that mother is the best person to assist the baby in language development.

Croons and lullabies take precedence in the first three months because of their ability to relax and bring a sense of security to your infant. From then on you can draw on a wealth of baby songs and rhymes. These include dandling songs, play songs, tickling and leg-waggling rhymes, knee-dancing, foot-patting and body-touching rhymes, along with the better known toe and finger rhymes. All of these rhymes help the baby's mobility, ability, enjoyment, and provide the necessary variety of speech patterns.

[3] Day, B. and Liley, M., *The Secret World of Baby (New York; Random House, 1968).*
[4] *Chamberlain, D.B., Consciousness at Birth* San Diego, California, U.S.A., 1983.
[5] Research carried out at the City Hospital, Elmhurst, N.Y., U.S.A. by Dr. Salk, 1962.
[6] Studies in Mother-Infant Interaction, W.S. Condon, N.Y. Academy Press N.Y., 1977.
[7] Article in the Sunday Observer, London, June 23, 1974.

Music programs are important because nowadays the majority of mothers haven't grown up in a musical environment and do not know what songs or rhymes to sing to their babies. In the old days, when families were larger, older sisters or grannies were usually available to play and sing to the new baby and pass on these songs. Now, while mothers have many more modern conveniences, they lack this type of musical background.

In educational institutions involving young infants and babies, games and songs should be sung whenever the baby is picked up or changed.[8] When babies are in their cots they should be able to listen to a lullaby until they go to sleep. When they wake up they should be talked to and encouraged to participate in a variety of activities to enhance their perceptual development.

Babies are selective and will only participate in "learning" as long as their attention is challenged. Such a challenge needs to be met by the mother or mother substitute. An enriched environment stimulates the babies curiosity and leads to greater participation by the mother to satisfy the baby's demands. On the other hand, deprivation, including the lack of auditory stimulation, increases the infant's chance of apathy, and can lead to withdrawal and passivity. An infant who turns inward is less able to reach for the outside help that is essential if she is to develop. If the passive baby is deprived in other ways she will, by the time she reaches preschool age, probably need a good deal of specialized help.

Once the neonate period (one month) is past, there is no need to be concerned with chronological age, because it will not necessarily correspond to the musical age of your baby. What *is* important is to see that the enrichment program of sound and movement keeps pace with, or possibly one jump ahead of, the musical capabilities of your baby.[9]

In taking into account your baby's rhythmic responses, you should be aware that each baby, as a human, has its own natural rhythm. When this rhythm is disturbed the baby may become over-excited, unwell, or frightened. She can be helped back to her own rhythm by pattings and croonings. To do this you must follow her own excited pattern and then gradually bring her down to her normal pattern. Interestingly enough, this rhythmic approach was used long ago by Sufi Inayat Khan (1882-1927) who made the comment, "Relaxation comes through an even rhythm, comfort and calm surroundings."

Just as Vivaldi and Mozart have helped to relax a four to five-month-old fetus[10], so instrumental music can be helpful when you have to deal with a young baby who might be screaming from an emotional upset. Perhaps her mother has left her, or she has been badly frightened by some unusual noise or movement. Talking or singing is often of no avail, but try a "counter startle" technique by playing some recorded music, or present her with the striking and beautiful sound of a glass mobile, or the sound of the keys of the piano, or the plucking of a guitar string, and the screaming will stop almost instantly. Then you can move in with the reassurance of body and sound in a cuddle and lullaby.

[8] Developmental Methods of Physical Care Routines with Infants: Department of Applied Psychology, Ontario Institute of Education, 1972.
[9] Some recent advantages in the study of early deprivation: A.D.B. Clarke and A.M. Clarke, Journal of Child Psychology and Psychiatry, 1960, pp 1-26.

Your baby needs an individual voice on which to pattern her speech and in her early months she should not be confused by too many voices, for all voices differ. Mother is obviously the right person for this patterning, but if mother is not available there should be one person she can feel attached to who will take responsibility for her sound sessions (this would apply in a prolonged daycare situation or in an orphanage). Because children usually pattern their voice on their mother's voice, it is quite common to find a well-established "family" voice among children. Research has also shown that a baby's first cry can be matched with its mother's voice.[11]

By the time your baby is a year old, her emotions can be channeled and expressed by encouraging her to play with simple percussion instruments — rattles, bells, tone blocks, drums, pan lids, small pans — anything that can be held, makes a lively sound, and is not dangerous.

She can enjoy participating in play songs such as, "Pat-A-Cake-" or "Peek-A-Boo". Some of the earlier play and body songs can become question songs, such as, "Where is mummy's nose?", "Where is baby's nose?" Because of your baby's boundless energy dandling songs such as, "Dance-A-Baby-Diddy" or "Dance to your Daddy" (songs which aim at tiring baby out before she goes to bed), are much enjoyed.

During the first year of growth, requisite physical skills have been acquired by repetition (how to get her finger in her mouth, how to turn over, how to use her voice). By repeating the sounds she hears and adding new sounds when she is ready, she will learn to speak in the same way.

Although at this stage we may understand very little of what she says, it is clear your baby understands much of what we say to her. This can be seen by her reactions to our "no no" or "dinner time" when she makes a beeline for her high chair. Just as she has learned about her physical environment through feeling everything, first with her mouth, then with her hands, feet, and whole body. So she learns about her sound environment by imitating and absorbing sound; and because every sound is a new experience, she remembers what she hears.

Each baby is likely to have its own way of learning and this should be kept in mind when planning an enrichment program. The "feeling" baby will spend longer feeling everything, and may find a variety of musical toys with a variety of textures, an endless source of delight. The "muscular development" baby will enjoy music best when she is moving, and will find lively and rhythmical records very entertaining. The listening baby will respond to voices, songs, music, and any new sounds. She will actually "listen" briefly and try very hard to participate in some way if her family or friends are making music together. The seeing baby will concentrate on looking at everything and will respond to sound by watching the mother's expression and the shape of her lips when speaking.

---

[10] Observation on certain aspects of neonatal behavior in response to auditory stimuli: M. Clements Paper Fifth Inter. Congress of Psychosomatic Obstetrics and Gynecology.
[11] *Acta Paediatrica,* H. Truby and J. Lind Scandinavica Supplement, 1965.

From 18 months to two years, your baby enters a new period; although she is not yet past what Piaget calls the sensormotor period, a period when "long practice of pure action is necessary to construct the sub-structure of speech."[12] Because she will now be walking, singing games such as, "Ring-A-Round-A-Rosy" or "Here we go round the Mulberry Bush" can be part of the program. She can now enjoy simple books. Let her look at a nursery rhyme book while you sing it to her so that she can absorb both the music and the pictures. At this stage, it is worth writing out a series of very simple songs, using large notes and Sol-Fa[13] symbols, to help her recognize that music is a tangible thing that can be looked at as well as sung:

Hello **Hee-Haw** **Stand up** **Rain is Falling Down** **Sunny Day**

D D¹ S D S D¹ M M R R D S S L

Your baby enters the world of organized ideas or concepts through speech. Her ability to speak plays an important part in identifying parts of her body, discriminating between right and left, and becoming aware of the dimensions of space. (As she is only just beginning to speak, there should be no stress on right or left concepts in the singing games or in any of her movements to music.)

Although there are still many concepts which will cause your baby difficulty, they can be dealt with easily and unobtrusively through music: "big and small", "high and low", "colour recognition", "different shapes" and "the use of space". She can be a big liner, a ferry boat, or a little tug. She can hear the voice of daddy bear, mummy bear, or baby bear. If colours are used with the Sol-Fa sounds, she can find the colour which matches the sound, or match sound with the colour. If she is given a round shape — a drum, she can be asked to play the instrument which corresponds with the shape she is shown; or the person playing with her can play the instrument and ask her to find the matching shape. Use of colour with the shapes adds another dimension. A feeling for space can be encouraged through movement. "Put your arms out and see what space you have. Move in upper space, middle and lower space. This is a big space, try to spread out and use all this space when you move." (All these suggestions should be shown when spoken.)

Babies find differences in timbre one of the easier things to hear. When she listens to the sound of a big drum, a tone block, or bells, she can easily find and imitate the sounds if played again, without her seeing the instrument.[14] From imitating rhythms (echo clapping) she learns to imitate and remember. By listening to a variety of beautiful melodies many times, she will remember them and they can console her in later life if she is lonely or in pain. Perhaps the most valuable experience is that she has learned to listen and through listening, to concentrate.

[12] *The Child and Reality* Jean Piaget, F. Muller Ltd., U.K., 1974.
[13] See subsequent chapters.
[14] *Newer Concepts of Pitch, the Loudness and the Timbre of Musical Tone* H. Fletcher, I. Franklin Institute (200) 1935, pp. 405-429.

Before she is two the baby will be ready socially to enjoy other children. A program including other mothers and babies will contribute to her musical progress and overall development. From twenty to twenty-four months old, many babies love to join in the singing while a certain proportion of them will be able to "sing a tune."[15] Often they make up their own songs, sometimes using a melody that they know and making up their own words, sometimes using words they know but making up their own melody. At this stage they can play a variety of rhythmic patterns on the drum or rhythm sticks. They also like trying to imitate sounds they hear, and are aware of loud and soft music and fast and slow music.

Many mothers need professional musical help to start with but nearly every mother who is willing to enlarge her musical experience and improve her singing voice by practicing, will find that by providing a musical environment she will build a closer relationship with her baby and enrich her own appreciation of music.

---

[14] *Newer Concepts of Pitch, the Loudness and the Timbre of Musical Tone* H. Fletcher, I. Franklin Institute (200) 1935, pp. 405-429.
[15] *Perceptual Shifts in the Auditory Information Processing of Young Children,* D. Sergeant and S. Roch, Psychology of Music, Vol. 1 No. 2, 1973.

[1] Stone, L. J. and Murphy, L. B. (eds.) *The Competent Infant* (London; Tavistock Publishers, 1974).
[2] Truby, H. M., *Child Language* World Journal of the International Linguistic Assoc., 1975.

CHAPTER 4

Voice: the instrument we all possess

Your child's love of singing grows from his delight in all kinds of different sounds, particularly the sounds he discovers he can make with his own voice, and the sounds he hears his mother making with her voice. He quickly distinguishes between happy and angry sounds, loud startling sounds, and gentle, melodious sounds. He loves to imitate mother as she sings at bath time, at dressing or undressing time, at bed time, or in the car when they are travelling.

It is sad when mothers do not feel they sing well enough to sing to their children. Almost any singing is better than none at all. Your baby does not expect or want a beautifully produced voice; he expects and wants a comforting sound. Nothing is so beautiful or so satisfying to a young child as his mother's voice. Father's voice is very satisfying too, but it can't replace mother's. It is merely an added bonus.

Nursery school teachers should try to find time to sing to the children as well as with them. All young children love to be sung to, just as they love to be told stories. For both the child's pleasure and your sense of confidence, you want your voice to sound as pleasant as possible. So here are some suggestions on how to improve the quality of your voice.

First of all, in order to sing easily, you must breathe properly. Try taking a deep breath: one that will expand the rib cage and the diaphragm without lifting the shoulders. The ribs must not collapse, therefore, an upright position is necessary. This does not mean that you have to stand, although that makes it easier; an upright sitting position is equally good. The breath must be controlled so it does not come out all at once; this will enable you to sing to the end of a musical phrase, such as "Lavender's blue, dilly dilly, Lavender's green". To practice good breathing, stand and breathe in slowly while you count to four. Now breathe out while you count to four. (Notice that your ribs expand at the back as well as sideways). When you sing, open your mouth wide (for how else can your voice get out?) Make good use of your tongue, lips and even teeth when you are singing words containing double ee's such as "meet". As your voice rises, the tongue tends to rise, blocking the back of the throat. This makes singing high notes feel difficult. Try to keep the tongue flat, or stick it out every now and then to see whether the back of your throat is really clear

ALLY BALLY

Ostinato (Melodic) Ostinato (Rhythmic)

Lullaby

Clap on first and third beats. First to the right and then to the left.

Verse 2 Seven o'clock now, my little man Off to bed as quick as you can
When you wake with the morning light I'll give you a stick of candy.

FOR DAY'S WORK AND WEEK'S WORK

Hebridean Folk Song

Song with chorus. (The teacher can sing the verse and the children the chorus.)

Verse 2
A kitten and a lilac bush- Bridal white and tall
And later crimson ramblers against a granite wall.
Verse 3
I have passed your railings when you never knew
To people who have gardens I give my thanks to you.

In order to become more conscious of the freedom of your tongue, sing this exercise on any note: fa, la, la, la, la, la, la, la, (♩ ♫ ♫ ♫ ♩). Say "Peter Piper picked a peck of pickled peppercorns" to become more familiar with your lips. To become more aware of the sounding board made by your teeth, sing "me" with the teeth together.

Always try to keep your voice above your breath (i.e. imagine that the breath in your rib cage is an inflated air pillow and your voice sings on top of this, never sinking down into the pillow). All inhalation must be silent. Otherwise it means that the breath is rasping on the vocal cords which damages them.

Project your voice (i.e. imagine that you want someone at the other end of the room to hear what you are singing). This does not mean loud singing; it is the quality, not the quantity that carries.

Finally, when you sing always try to produce a beautiful and alive sound. Since it is very difficult to hear your own voice, use a tape recorder. When you play the tape back, do not be too discouraged; your voice always seems to sound worse on a tape than it does in real life!

ECHO SONG

Traditional

As I looked out my win-dow, to see what I could see. I saw a big fat Ro-bin, he said hel-lo to me. Hel-lo, (hel-lo.) How are you? (How are you?) I'm just fine (I'm just fine) And pleased to see you too. (And pleased to see you too.)

34

J'ENTENDS LE MOULIN

French Canadian folk song

J'en-tends le mou-lin ti-que ti-que ta-que J'en-tends le mou-lin ta-que.

Mon père a fait ba- tir mai-son J'en-tends le mou-lin ta-que.

L'a fait ba-tir à trois pi-gnons ti-que, ta- que ti-que, ta-que.

(I hear the mill wheel turning, my father builds himself a house, he has three carpenters to keep.)

Use as a question and answer song, play the ti-que ta-que on rhythm sticks.

JOHNNIE WRITES:

Imitative Song

1. John-nie writes, writes, writes, John-nie writes, writes, writes, all day long. John-nie writes all day long.

2. Sus-ie skips, skips, skips, Sus-ie skips, skips, skips, **etc.**

3. Moth-er cooks, cooks, cooks, Moth-er cooks, cooks, cooks, **etc.**

ECHO SONG   Traditional

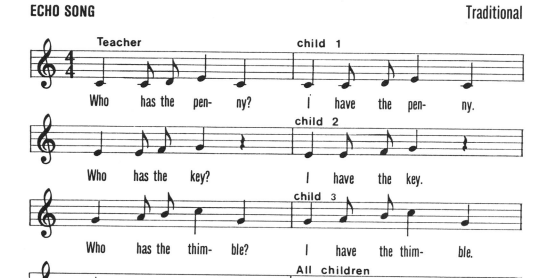

Any items may be used instead of the ones here

This song can also be used to teach the children to listen.
By asking those who do not hold an item to close their eyes
and guess which child is singing.

The words that you sing are made up of vowels; **a, e, i, o, u,** which are the easiest sounds to sing; dipthongs: **ai, ae,** etc.; I's and consonants: **t, d, p,** etc. Consider the beauty and character of words: the bright rich sound of gold, the smooth sad sound of silver, or the singing **"m"** of mother.

Remember that the more you know about your own voice and use it, the more you will enjoy singing and the more the children will enjoy hearing you. If you continue to listen to the sound you make and avoid forcing or smothering your voice, it will become easier to sing in tune and make a song sound the way you want it to sound.

I know these arguments will not convince some mothers and teachers. They will still insist they cannot sing because "they have no ear, they cannot hold a tune, or their voice is ugly or so soft that it will never carry". Some people certainly have more difficulty in singing than others; however, everyone has a voice and it is through a combination of thinking, listening, and practicing that almost every voice can be developed. Often, the belief that you cannot sing is based on being told, as a child, that you had no voice. Or sometimes it is because no one in your family has been concerned with singing and as a result you have never tried to use your voice. You are, therefore, very self-conscious when you do try to use it and think you are much worse than you are.

Today, because we hear so much good singing on records and on the radio, we are much more conscious of our own vocal short-comings. But don't be discouraged. Children do not expect a professionally-trained voice. Quite often this feeling that you cannot hold a tune or make your voice carry lies in your own mind. Sing and the children will enjoy you and the more you sing, the better you will sing! There is no area where people differ more than in their response to music. So console yourself with the thought that, although singing is important and you may never sing very well, you can contribute just as much through dancing, playing an instrument, dramatizing music, or discovering with children the pleasure of listening to music.

Children (particularly around the ages of 5 and 6) are genuinely interested in singing techniques. Take time to try certain things. They can feel how they breathe when they make the sound of the wind: Whoo, whoo, whoo; they can feel their lips move when they say: pitter, pitter, patter; they can wiggle their tongues to the fa, la, la, la, la, exercise and enjoy trying to roll their r's. Children can feel both their tongues and their lips in the deeper clip clop sound made by horses' hooves; they can experience the soft beauty of the sound they make when they sing "lulla-lulla lullaby"; and they can project their voices in a long "cooee".

There may be some excuse for an uncertain voice; there is no excuse for poor diction. Children learn to speak clearly by listening to clear articulation. In much the same way,they learn to make pleasing sounds by listening to well sung melodies. If you find, inspite of practice, you cannot do this, play a song or melody on the xylophone, the recorder, or on the piano. In this way the children hear the melody correctly the first time.

Children with speech difficulties (and there are many) find it harder to learn a song. When they sing it we find that they are not saying many of the letters correctly. I always remember one little boy who, looking at one of the chime bars, said "Don't 'oo fink dat is wavver wike a wikkle wareoplane? He was not quite three. He really sounded rather adorable and he was adorable, however, he really could not say his "th's", "r's", "l's" and "t's" and what is sweet at two or three is less sweet at five or six!

Some children also have trouble with "s" and ending consonants like "d" and "t". There are many songs which concentrate on these letters, e.g. Mary had a little lamb, (L), Ring around the Rosy (R), This is the way we clap our hands (TH) and (H). Singing songs that they enjoy, getting them to listen to the words as you sing them, and encouraging them to repeat some of the words which do not sound quite right, is a tremendous help. Rhymes also help, and a funny one like Moses* is excellent for (S) and (R).

It is not a good idea to concentrate on the child with speech difficulties as this usually makes him anxious and self-conscious. Instead, get all the children to try rolling their r's; then ask them to put their tongues a little bit out and blow over it and say "th"; sometimes they say "fh" and need to be shown that "f" comes on the front of the lips when they blow and "t" is further back.

*" Moses supposes his tosies are roses
But Moses supposes erroneously!
For nobody's tosies are posies of roses
Which Moses supposes his tosies to be."

PITTER-PATTER

Barbara Cass-Beggs

Pit-ter pat-ter, pit-ter pat-ter, lis-ten to the rain.

Pit-ter pat-ter, pit-ter pat-ter, on the window pane.

Drop-ping drop-ping, drop-ping drop-ping drop-ping on the ground

Drop-ping drop-ping, drop-ping drop-ping, lis-ten to the sound.

For Diction

They can also be shown that in order to say "l" the tongue has to be behind the front teeth. I find that children think these exercises are very funny and love trying to make all these sounds correctly.

This kind of letter practice can be followed by tongue twisters, which children always enjoy. Sometimes I ask how many children can say HAT and MAD and let me hear the T and D. All of them of course want to show me how clever they are! Then we see how many words we can think of which rhyme with HAT and MAD'

I once had a little Japanese boy in one of my classes whose speech was so poor that we all had difficulty in understanding him. Luckily he loved singing and never minded repeating a song if I suggested that I had not heard all the words. Sometimes after class I would ask him if he would like to sing one of his favourite songs. As he could not usually remember all the words, this gave us an opportunity to go over some of the words, emphasizing their pronunciation. By the end of the term we could all understand him. As a result, he was a much happier boy.

Apart from songs which we may select to deal with speech difficulties, the choice of children's songs is very important. When selecting songs certain qualities should be checked. They should be short and simple and have an interesting rhythm or pattern, a balanced shape and an attractive melody. By an attractive melody I mean a melody that moves in a pleasant curving line and has some distinctive character. If you sing the nursery rhyme "Lavenders Blue" you will find that it meets these requirements, as do many of the nursery rhymes and folk songs.

LAVENDER'S BLUE

Nursery Rhyme

Lav- en- der's blue Dil-ly Dil-ly, Lav- en- der's green,

When I am king Dil-ly Dil-ly you shall be Queen.

Categories from which suitable songs can be chosen include nursery rhymes, folk songs, singing games, traditional songs and contemporary songs composed for children. As soon as you know a number of songs from each of these categories, you should classify them for easy reference under such headings as: action songs, animal songs, finger (and toe) songs, play songs, idea songs, language songs, made-up songs, mood songs, nonsense songs, personal contact songs, quiet songs, special occasion songs and weather or seasonal songs. For children who find singing difficult, echo songs or songs with an easy chorus are useful because they can imitate what the teacher sings.

When you come to teach a song, there are certain things to be kept in mind if we are to be effective.

- You and the children must be ready to sing. It's no good starting if Jane's sock has come off and she is trying to put it on or Tim has suddenly discovered that he has a toy car in his pocket! Apart from distractions, you and the children want to feel comfortable.

- Your face must be level with the children's faces, so that they can see your expression and the movement of your lips. You need to see all their faces, because if they are looking *at* you, you will have their attention. A circle on the floor is perhaps the best, as chairs impede movement, are noisy and make it all rather formal.

- If the song is about something unknown, describe what it is and tell them something about it before you sing the song. (The notes accompanying folk song collections are very helpful in this respect).

- The first time sing the song alone, with good articulation so that lip reading is possible. The second time everyone can be asked to sing and the third time (or the second time if preferred), the children can clap the pattern of the song. If there is still some uncertainty about the words, they can be repeated line by line with the children and it is helpful to say them according to the rhythmic pattern.

- Finally, the song can be sung again, this time expecting the children to do *all* the singing. Three or four times through is about enough for any song unless the children are very anxious to sing it again

Any actions which accompany songs must be there when the song is first sung, for if the actions are not so much a part of the song that one cannot resist putting them in, they are probably unnecessary.

As a rule not more than five or six songs should be sung without a break for some movement, and it is a good idea to plan the order of the selected songs. You can begin with a song which is either linked with what the children have just been doing, or a song which is known and liked, for the purpose of the first song is to draw the children together into a group.

The second song can be a new song and the third might demand some action or participation, such as "Sing a Song of Sixpence", where the children can play the parts of the king, the queen, the maid and the blackbird and finish up by all flying around as blackbirds.

Sing a Song of Sixpence

Nursery Rhyme

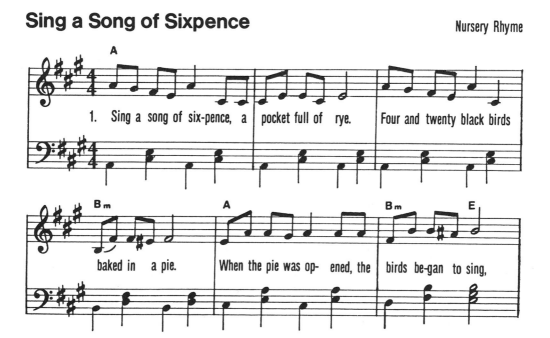

Was-n't that a dain-ty dish to set be- fore the king?

2. The King was in his counting house counting out his money.
The Queen was in the parlour eating bread and honey
The maid was in the garden hanging out the clothes
Along came a black-bird and pecked off her nose!

The fourth song can be another new one, perhaps a language song and you can close with a song which they all know, so that the signing period ends on a relaxed note.

Quite often songs provoke discussion and a song period can be one of the most rewarding musical experiences.

Once, before singing a lullaby, I asked who had a baby brother or sister at home to sing to, Beatrice said, "My mummy has a baby in her tummy, can I sing to my mummy?" We all decided that this was a good idea and when Beatrice added with pride, "You know, I came out of my mummy's tummy too," there was a joyful chorus of "So did I, so did I!" from the rest of the class.

Another time we had been singing "I love little pussy", and before singing we had each picked up an imaginary pussy to hold on our knee while we sang. Each child had described her pussy cat and at the end of the song, during a short silence before we put our pussies down and told them to run away. Betty, aged four, looked up, sighed regretfully, and said, "That was a nice pussy cat, wasn't it?"

Children do not need to sit in one particular position, all you need is their attention (although if they lie on their tummies I tell them that they cannot sing like that because the air is pressed out of their ribs).

"Someday," my daughter said, "I'm not going to sing in nursery school."

"Why?" I said, knowing that she loved to sing.

"When we sing we have to cross our feet," she said, "So some day I'm not going to sing."

It has been mentioned earlier that parents and teachers are sometimes worried because children sing off-key (something which often occurs with young children). This can be due to a number of things, including psychic inhibitions, or under-developed vocal chords; the most common causes, however, are poor listening, lack of practice, or listening to someone who does not produce a musical tone with clarity.

One thing which helps children to sing in tune is to start the song at a comfortable pitch. A small child has a limited range and sings at a lower pitch than is usually realized, (B flat to B flat and not higher than D-D). Songs that are too high or too low, (although the tendency is to pitch them too high) cause difficulty because, although the child may hear the sounds, he cannot reproduce them accurately. It is important for a child to hear the starting note of a song, for singing off pitch can also be caused by uncertainty about the starting note, which in turn leads to uncertainty about the pitch of the song.

Children learn songs by ear and imitate those who sing them. For example, in Saskatchewan I was accused of turning out Western Canadian children with English accents! However, as has already been noted, it is vital for the music teacher to be able to sing in tune and articulate clearly!

There are two types of pitch: "Perfect pitch", which means that the exact pitch of the note can be identified and reproduced without any outside reference and "relative pitch", which means if one note is identified, others can be played or sung. The term "tone deaf" is used when the pitch of a sound cannot be identified or sung. This has nothing to do with "deafness" as such. The person hears the sound but cannot identify what it is and cannot reproduce that sound vocally. Very few people are tone deaf, although a lot of people claim to be. Genuine tone deafness is rarely cured, but "fancied" tone deafness is cured by learning to listen, to concentrate, to produce a musical tone in the right way and sing with other people who sing in tune. Genuine tone deafness is something like colour blindness, except that colour blindness is a sex-linked hereditary characteristic transmitted by the female to the male and is rare in women.

Pitch games as well as songs are very useful in developing a child's ability to hear and later produce sounds of varying pitch and they can be used in a variety of ways, and at a variety of times. As I use them primarily in learning how to read music they are included in that chapter

In the meantime there is nothing like singing to encourage more singing, so here are some of the songs I have mentioned in this chapter. Luckily, we have so many excellent song books (see book list) that it is not necessary to include more than a certain number of examples.

Apart from a few songs whose primary aim is to help the child to read or overcome some speech difficulty, all songs should be musically worth while in themselves, so that they can be continually enjoyed, even when the child is no longer a child!

42

OH COME MY TOP (Ah si mon moine) French Canadian folk song   (English words, Barabara Cass Beggs)

1. Oh come my top will you dance with me, O come my top will you dance with me, so very hap-py I be. so ve-ry hap py I shall be.

Spin my top come spin now, skip my top come skip now, I love my top to dance with me, so ve-ry hap-py I shall be.

2. Off we go on our merry-go-round. Off we go on our merry-go-round.
Our feet can scarcely touch the ground, as we go whirling round and round.

3. Gee up horsie, whoa there. Gee up horsie, whoa there!
We love to ride on the merry-go-round. It's quite the nicest thing in town.

As "moine" (monk), also means "top", It seems reasonable to turn this into a top song, and as it is such a jolly melody a merry-go-round fits equally well.
(Ternary Form A.B.A.)

Learning through Movement

Movement of any kind is so much a part of any child that it is natural for your baby to want to move to music. She was moving rhythmically in her mother's womb and as a baby she has continued to stretch, turn, wiggle and later on, crawl and creep. Your child does not need to be persuaded to wiggle her toes, wave her arms or sway up and down; these are things she naturally wants to do and they are a vital part of her physical and mental development. She belongs in a world of natural rhythm; her mother's lullabies, the rocking of her cradle, the opening and closing of curtains, the sound of different people walking. She is always discovering new ways to move and is triumphant when she finds, after long practice, that she can grasp her rattle, her toes or her mother's hair!

Because moving is so much part of every child it is a good idea to start a music class with some form of rhythmic movement. The type of movement chosen will depend upon what stage the children are at, and what they have been doing before they came to music class. It is always useful to do something which will link the child with what she has been doing previously.

If she has come directly from home we can ask whether she walked to class? ran? came by car or bus? or was pushed in her stroller? Children can imitate various types of locomotion to the accompaniment of suitable music, which can range from a simple drum beat to a piano accompaniment or recorded music.

If they have come from active out-door play, they may prefer some token exercise such as wiggling fingers and toes, clapping their hands, or nodding their heads, just to get them calmed down and settled.

If they have been sitting still for some time then a variety of musical games can be initiated which can include crawling and creeping, (a worm or a snail), bouncing, (a ball), hopping, (a frog or a bunny), galloping, (a horse), jumping, (a kangaroo), spinning, (a top), bending, (an elephant waving his trunk), sliding, (a skater). Walking or running could be geared to drum rhythms which can include loud and soft, and quick and slow rhythms.

The weather and season changes provide us with a wonderful variety of movements. In the fall we can rake, catch, roll in, or kick the leaves. We can pick fruit and gather berries. In the winter we can skate, slide, ski, or build snowmen. In the spring we can splash in puddles and look for the first flowers. A song like "It's Blowing" can suggest wind, rain, snow, puddles, ice, fog or any weather condition which prevails at the moment.

Locomotion provides another popular form of movement — cars, buses, ships, planes and games such as bouncing and throwing balls, skipping, or flying kites, are popular ways of moving.

Children can listen to music which walks like a giant, gallops like a pony, tiptoes like a fairy or a pussy cat or sways like the branches of a tree. They can tell us what they think the music is doing and then imitate it.

Different people can be imitated by different ways of walking — a policeman, Bat-man, mummy shopping, a soldier. Children can also do a number of different jobs such as digging and raking in the garden, polishing and sweeping the house, sawing and hammering in the workshop.

Stories can be created — such as in a forest, where the trees sway and bend in the wind, where plants grow, animals roam around and a family arrives to look for a nice place to have a picnic. A circus also provides an excellent story, particularly if there is one in town at the time. There can be a Ring Master with a whip, clowns and animals and performers on the high wires: in fact, any characters suggested by the children.

It is always helpful to classify the different types of movement that you are using so that you are aware of exercising all the parts of a child's body, including her gross and fine motor movement. There are head movements including eyes and mouth; arm, hand and finger movements leg, feet and toe movements and whole body movements. There are a variety of directions in which we can move up/down, backwards/forwards, under/over, in a circle. There are also many methods of moving; slowly/quickly, quietly/loudly, heavily/lightly.

Remember that all children have their own natural way of moving which can be discovered by watching them, and this can be directed and utilized, for it is basic to their rhythmic response. Often children who are ill, nervous, or very timid, produce jerky and uncomfortable movements. In moving to music you should encourage these children to relax, move more freely and make use of every part of their body. Today many children are tense, and need to learn how to relax, so you should provide many opportunities for them to become floppy rag dolls, collapsing air balloons, melting snowmen or soft wiggly worms!

In all rhythmic movement children need to be conscious of the space in which they move, both in relation to themselves and the other children; and because space, like pitch, can be thought of in three levels, high middle and low, their rhythmic movements can complement their pitch games. Naturally many songs lend themselves to movement; clapping, or moving to an ostinato, as in *"who has seen the wind"* or following the directions of the words in action as in *"Off we go on our merry-go-round"*.[1]

Certain types of songs such as, *"Head, Shoulders, Knees, Toes"*, actually tell the children how to move. However, these types of songs should only be used occasionally for they are very stylized and not very creative.

Rhythmic movements associated with body percussion provide a lot of fun and inventiveness, and children are surprised to discover how many different sounds and movements can be made just by using their own bodies. Interesting sounds can be made with the lips, tongue, tummy or behind, as well as hands and feet — for example, if we body percuss a nursery rhyme such as "Humpty Dumpty", we can smack our head for line one, slide our hands from our head to our feet, finishing up with a stamp on "fall" for line two, make a galloping rhythm on our hips for line three, and shake our wrists helplessly, finishing up with a clap on the word "again" for line four.

It is always a good idea to end an active or exciting session on a quiet note, such as a tip toe march or the silent flight of a glider. If the quietness is part of the thing that the children are doing, it evokes a perfectly natural response and we do not need to tell them that we want them to be quiet and settle down for the next musical experience.

WHO HAS SEEN THE WIND ?

Music: Spanish Folk　　Words: Christina Rosetti

1. See page 42 for music example.

Ostinato: piano or chime bars.

The rhythmic and melodic ostinato can be used together or separately.

IT'S BLOWING

Barbara Cass Beggs

It's blow- ing, it's blow- ing it's blow- ing all a- round ——— it's blow- ing, it's blow- ing it makes a win- dy sound.

In later verses it can rain, snow, freeze-etc.

LOOBY LOO

Singing Game Traditional

Here we dance loo- by loo, Here we dance loo- by light, Here we dance loo- by loo, All on a Sat-tur-day night.

2. We wave our arms in
We wave our arms out
We wave them in the middle again
And turn ourselves about

3. We put our leg in
4. We put our head in
5. We put our nose in
6. We put our whole selves in

Group children in pairs for such well known songs as "Row, Row, Row Your Boat" or "See, Saw, Marjorie Daw" or in groups for a train song such as "I've Been Working on the Railway" or "The Noble Duke of York", and they always enjoy making the same movements at the same time in singing games such as "Looby Loo" or "Hokey Pokey".

HOKEY POKEY

Traditional

You put your right foot in you put your right foot out you put your right foot in and you shake it all a-bout you do the ho-key po-key and you turn a-round. That's what it's all a-bout bout.

Oh ho-key po-key po-key Oh ho-key po-key po-key Oh ho-key po-key po-key That's what it's all a-bout

VIOLETTE

Un deux trois quatre cinq six sept, Vi-o-ette, Vi-o-lette Un deu trois quatre cinq six sept. Vi-o-lette en bi-cy-clette.

Children lie on their backs and bicycle with their legs.

PAPILLONS VOLES

French Nursery Rhyme

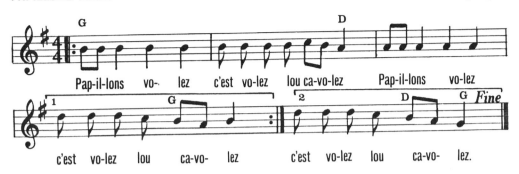

Pap-il-lons vo- lez c'est vo-lez lou ca-vo-lez Pap-il-lons vo-lez

c'est vo-lez lou ca-vo- lez c'est vo-lez lou ca-vo- lez.

Children fly round like butterflies (use coloured scarves), or
make fluttering movements with their hands.

When they are around five or six, it is interesting to see whether they can communicate with each other through movement (mime) "come here", "go away", "sit down", "stand up". Very simple charades can be played with one half of the group choosing a word and acting it out and the other half guessing what it is, for example Bat-man for a person or necklace for a thing. This kind of game improves their vocabulary and their spelling.

In spite of the fact that the majority of young children enjoy moving to music, it is not unusual to find a perfectly normal group of two or three year olds who want to *sit* and have no intention of committing themselves to spontaneous movement of any kind! It may be because they are nervous or self-conscious; or because their main emphasis has shifted from senso-motor activity to perceiving, questioning, and enlarging their vocabulary or it may be because they associate this kind of movement with "being a baby". (After all, grownups do not skip or run, they walk or sit!)

When it is obvious that we are faced with such a group who feel "sitting is safest", I follow our opening song with some very *organized* movement, for a framework gives them a sense of security with no loss of dignity. For example, there is usually a good response if I ask them to "do what my drum is doing", particularly if it starts off by saying, "stand up", and then continues with marching or walking.

This movement can change to running, stamping, jumping or tiptoeing, and it will not be long before the children are suggesting other things that the drum can do, such as hopping, sliding or galloping. By the time the children have reached the stage of taking turns on the drum themselves, and telling it what to do, they are well on their way to forgetting their fears and are ready to enjoy more imaginative types of movement.

Singing games provide another excellent way of getting shy or inhibited children to join in, for there is the added security of "holding hands" and the fun of singing a song together, which with any luck they may already know.

Sometimes just "walking" will get everyone going. "How does your mummy walk?" (illustrate) "Does a bunny walk?" "No, he hops."

"Well, let's all hop like bunnies. Let's go for a quick walk, a slow walk, a walk when we are carrying something heavy, a tip-toe walk."

The ability to hear and maintain a steady beat or tempo is a necessary part of all music training and assists the child in making accurate motor responses. It is surprising how many new learning experiences are acquired through music and movement, for all concepts need to be experienced before they are understood, and movement can provide this experience.

"Come near enough to touch me" — "run to the far end of the room" (near and far). "Reach up high and pretend to pick an apple" — "reach down to pick up one which has fallen" (high and low) — "See how wide you can stretch your arms" — "now make a narrow space with your hands" (wide and narrow).

They become aware of their bodies and experience a sense of direction when we move in/out, up/down, left/right., In simple dance patterns which grow out of singing games, the children become aware of shape — a line, a circle, a square (see chapter on How the Arts Relate to Music). Awareness of shapes can also be helped by using percussion instruments; a round drum, a triangle, an oblong chime bar. Movement also contributes more than we realize to an increased vocabulary.

As we know from our study of the baby, perceptual motor skills are essential for the child's overall physical, mental and emotional development. Until a child is able to move easily and enjoy moving she will never feel truly free or able to relate to her environment. Relaxed and enjoyable movement brings with it a sense of togetherness and stability, and we cannot expect children to be able to express rhythmic patterns and shapes or changes in dynamics and expression until they have developed body awareness. To quote from **Learning through Movement** (see book list, Appendix II), "The optimal development of the child's musical and motor capacities is dependent on rhythmical sensitivity and responsiveness".

In summarizing, I would say that, just as we have found that the baby is pre-programmed for speech, but that speech needs to be triggered by someone talking to her; so children are programmed for movement, but need help in learning how to *begin* to move. Moving to music provides one of the most enjoyable and easy ways of helping them to master the essential co-ordinating skills.

REMINDERS: List of Suggested Movement Songs
1. If You're Happy and You Know It
2. Head and Shoulders, Knees and Toes
3. Ha, Ha, This-A-Way
4. Come and Follow Me in a Line
5. One Finger, One Thumb, Keep Moving
6. Punchinello
7. The Muffin Man
8. The Noble Duke of York
9. As I Was Walking Down the Street
10. I Have Lost My Little Partner

List of Suggested Singing Games
1. Looby Loo
2. Hokey Pokey
3. Mulberry Bush
4. This Is The Way We Clap Our Hands
5. The Farmer in the Dell
6. In and Out the Window
7. Blue Bird, Blue Bird,
8. When I was a Young Girl
9. I Sent a Letter to My Love
10. Sally Go Round the Sun

CHAPTER 6

Introducing your child to instruments

All kinds of instruments appeal to both babies and young children. They like to move close to the person or persons who are playing, to see how these sounds are made. Then, of course, they want to try the instruments themselves, and are somewhat frustrated when they find that bowing, plucking or blowing is much more difficult than it looks. This is why the piano and auto-harp are such friendly instruments, for even a baby can press down the keys of a piano, and two children can share an auto-harp with one pressing the buttons and the other using the plectrum on the strings.

In order to introduce the piano properly you should show the children its inside and how it works: the hammers that hit the strings, the dampers which prevent the strings from sounding. Show what happens when you press the "loud" (right) or "soft" (left) pedal, or the third "sustaining" pedal (on some makes of pianos). When you show the length and thickness of the strings, explain that these help determine the pitch of the notes, although the pitch of a vibrating string does not depend *only* on its length but on its tension and the material from which it is made. Further attention can be drawn to "vibration" by letting the children hear and feel the vibrations of a tuning fork or playing comb music, which involves blowing and singing through a piece of tissue paper placed over a comb. You can ask them if they have watched a piano tuner at work, and you can tune the auto-harp and show them how to tighten a string to make the sound higher.

The tuning of instruments becomes even more obvious when you come to the **string family,** and although they are not as easy to play as the piano and auto-harp, strings can be plucked and the children can draw the bow across the strings while you hold the instrument. Children enjoy listening to the violin and viola because of the voice-like quality of the sound, while I usually find that the cello is the *real* favourite, with its body-like shape and its deep resonant voice.

The **woodwind** family is somewhat less approachable, for it is more difficult for children to produce a sound on them. The treble recorder is probably the easiest of this group, and while trying to play it children can be shown that the pitch (the tuning of the wind instrument) depends not only on the disposition of the holes and the fingering but upon the pressure of the breath. If suitable music is chosen children will enjoy listening to the clarinet, flute or oboe, although for some children the oboe quality of sound is too intense and it worries them. The bassoon always strikes children as a difficult instrument to play, but nevertheless they will enjoy listening to suitably selected music, especially the humorous "Elephant" in Sain-Saëns "Carnival of the Animals". (Naturally you would draw attention to the double reed of the oboe and the way a flute player blows over rather than into the holes on the flute.)

The other group of wind instruments, the **brass** family, always fascinates children, and they can often, to their great delight, produce a sound on a cornet, a trumpet or a French horn. As they are usually intrigued by the *coils* of the French horn, you can explain that in order to produce the range of sound required, a very long tube would be necessary, and to avoid the complication of playing such a long length of tube, the tube is coiled up! You need to be somewhat careful when introducing the **brass** family as a few children are frightened by the size of the instruments and overwhelmed by the sound of them.

Moving now to instruments which are banged or shaken to produce a sound, we come to the **percussion** family. Percussion instruments are not "tuned" except for the drums which are tuned by tightening or slackening the drum skin. This family is very popular because the children can play almost any of them, and they can make a lovely noise! Here again you need to be careful as the "noise", particularly the sound of the timpani drums scare some children.

It is an excellent idea to introduce children to all these families of instruments so that they know what they look like and become aware of their varieties of tone colour. However, children like to *do* things themselves, and at this stage they cannot play many of these instruments, therefore, a selection of good quality percussion instruments, such as triangles, tamborines, bells, rattles, etc. should be provided. Although they are limited in scope, they can still introduce the children to a variety of sound, provide another dimension for teaching rhythm and pitch, and form an ideal source for imaginative listening games and extemporizing, so it is worthwhile taking them seriously. And it is worthwhile, however easy the instrument, to see that we provide instruments of good quality, which produce a good quality sound!

Before introducing the percussion instruments, which I like to do individually, we might consider a number of different ways in which they can be used both individually and in group work.

1. The *Orff Tambour* can be used to tell the children what to do in movement and rhythm. It provides an alternate voice to the teacher and the children can have turns using it to direct the class too.

2. *Rhythm Sticks* can be used in many different ways but their main use is to provide a substitute or change from clapping, for they enable the child to play a rhythmic pattern with clarity. (It is quite difficult for the really young child (two or three) to clap a rhythm precisely.)

3. *Drums, tone blocks and tambourines* can be used to provide an exciting aid to the teaching of *rhythm,* for example:[1]

DRUM	DRUM		DRUM
TONE BLOCK	TONE BLOCK	TAMBOURINE	TONE BLOCK

(The drum is held on the **a** *of Ta-***a***.*)Very soon one group of children can play the pulse of a song, while others play the pattern, for example[2]

PATTERN   PULSE

4. *Percussion instruments* in general, can suggest different aspects of pitch and colour; the drums low and perhaps dark in colour, the bells and triangles high and perhaps silver or yellow, and the tambourines and tone blocks roughly in the middle, sometimes described as brown.

5. The playing of percussion instruments can provide an excellent method of illustrating musical dynamics, (loud and soft, quick and slow and *phrasing* and form in music.)

6. The actual playing of the instruments (and children must be taught how to hold them correctly) helps a child's dexterity and co-ordination.

7. The instruments can also provide an alternative for children who do not enjoy singing. Quite often these are children who are good with their hands, but have greater difficulty in expressing themselves verbally.

8. The instruments can be used to accompany songs about instruments and such songs usually provide an opportunity for each individual instrument to play.[1] They can also be used to accompany choruses of songs, specific actions and sound words in songs, or create a special atmosphere for a song. (see song examples)

[1] Hot Cross Buns
[2] Polly Put the Kettle On

To help children to listen and concentrate here are five simple, but entertaining percussion games that you can use.

1. Find six similar tins or boxes, and put different items in each (peas, pebbles, rice, etc.). First let the children guess what is in them, then when they know, mix the boxes up and ask them again.

2. Ask a child to go to the end of the room and turn her back on the music group and close her eyes. Choose with the help of the children, 2, 3 or 4 instruments. Play each one twice. Ask the child to come and play the instruments in the order in which they were played. (Most children manage to remember up to three instruments, four is usually one too many).

3. Let the children decide something that they would like to do to each instrument: e.g., march to the drum, run to the bells, clap to the tone blocks, stand still to the cymbals. Play these instruments, varying their order behind a box or table where they are not seen, and watch how quickly the children can move in the correct way.

4. Everyone else closes his eyes while one child selects and plays an instrument. Whoever guesses what it is first, has the next turn to choose an instrument.

5. Tell them a simple story using a variety of instruments to illustrate the different characters or sounds. Then let the children take turns in making up a story using the instruments. (You will usually find that the story centres around the instrument in which they are most interested!)

[1] To the melody of "This Old Man" (a song for all the instruments).

1. Susie Brown, she played one
   She played the triangles and had fun.
   With a tinkle, tinkle, bing bang, rattle rattle strum,
   Everyone is having fun.

2. He played the drum and so can you (two)

3. She played the tambourine on her knee (three)

4. He played the tone blocks on the floor (four)

5. She played the cymbals, and made them come alive (five)

6. He played rhythms on the rhythm sticks (six)

7. On chime bars that sounded like chimes for heaven (seven)

8. He made all the rattles go shake shake shake (eight)

9. He played the bells and they sounded fine (nine)

10. All of you, please play ten,
    Please play your music over again
    With a tinkle tinkle, bing bang rattle rattle strum
    Everyone is having fun!
    (Add your own children's names and put in instruments that you are using).

Now let us turn to the introduction of the individual percussion instruments starting off with the easy ones such as bells and rattles.

As babies, the children probably played with both bells and rattles which are so easy to shake and make a pleasant and fairly quiet sound, so these can be used at the start with a song like "Shake Your Bells"* or along with rattles. For example "Ride a Cock Horse", which can be sung and then sung again while the first two lines are accompanied with rattles, and the second two lines with bells. Children find it fun if they can listen to, and play a variety of bells such as sheep bells, sleigh bells, temple bells, dinner bells, etc. They like to be told where the various bells come from, and they can play them in turn, and then together accompanied by some bell music. (I use extracts from the record "The Exotic Sounds of Bali"[3], as this introduces gamelin, metalaphones and xylophones which link the melodic and percussive instruments together and give the children an idea of the varieties of vocal colour which can be produced by quite simple instruments).

Different types of rattles can also be demonstrated in this way, and they too can have a special piece of music to accompany them. (As many North American Indian dances use rattles, an Indian dance tune can be used, such as "Micmac War Dance Song"[4], from *Folk Music from Nova Scotia.*)

Drums have great appeal and whenever possible you should introduce a number of different drums, particularly some of the African drums such as the Bongo or the Yoruba. Children can practice playing the drums (with very loose wrists) while listening to extracts from "Drums of the Yoruba of Nigeria"[5]. North American Indian drums which are less sophisticated than the African drums, but are used in similar ways, can also be introduced and both drums and rattles can be played during the short extract on Indian drumming from "'Songs of Saskatchewan"[6].

The drum session might also include some children dancing, while others play the drums. They can make up messages on the drums and write them in their books, for example "Come to our Feast.[7], ♩ ♫ ♩ "Sun Arise" from the Australian record, "Tie Me Kangaroo Down" makes a lovely ending to a drum session for this song introduces the wobble board, sticks, drums and voices, and the children can play along with it using rattles, drums and their rhythm sticks. Before leaving drums entirely, we should have a look at Steel Band drums, and listen to extracts from a recording such as "Steel Band Spectacular"[8]. However, the children need to see and try a drum, so if pos-

*Shake your bells
Shake your bells
Shake your bells today
Oh what fun it is to shake
To shake your bells today
etc.
To the melody of "Jingle Bells"
[3] Columbia GL 100 4
[4] Folkways Ethnic Library F. 4006
[5] Folkways Ethnic Library FE 4441
[6] Folkways Ethnic Library FE 4312
[7] A Child's Introduction to Musical Instruments Golden Records. LP101
[8] Capitol 6000 Service

sible try to get a small tourist-style steel drum (from Trinidad or Jamaica) and let the children try it and then accompany a song such as, "When I Think of Nice Girl Lisa".

From the Orff Tambour the children can see how some drums are tuned, and they can look at pictures of the timpani drums used in orchestras and listen to the timpani in No. 7 of "A Child's Introduction to Musical Instruments"[9].

LIZA

Jamacian Folk Song

Ev'- ry time me 'mem-ba Li-za wa-ta come a me eye.

W'en me tink' pon me nice girl Li-za wa-ta come a me eye.

Come back Li-za come back girl, wa-ta come a me eye.

Come back Li-za come back girl, wa-ta come a me eye.

STEEL DRUM ACCOMPANIMENT

Tambourines can be introduced next, for they are easy to hold and can be shaken like rattles or hit like drums. Triangles can follow tambourines or be introduced at the same time, for although they are more difficult for young children to manage, they enjoy their contrasting sound. The various tone blocks can be introduced at any time, on their own, or with the drums. I usually introduce sand blocks in a story when that kind of sound is needed, for example, "The little boy ran home from school; (rhythm sticks), and wiped his feet on the mat; (sand blocks). Castanets are really too difficult for young children to manage, but those on a handle are quite easy, and can be classified and played with the tone blocks. (They also make excellent duck sounds).

[9] Columbia GL 10040

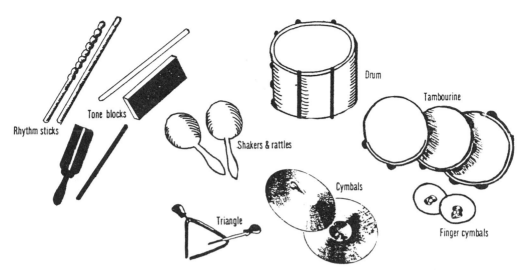

Rhythm sticks

Tone blocks

Shakers & rattles

Drum

Tambourine

Triangle

Cymbals

Finger cymbals

I do not use cymbals at all with children under four, for they are difficult to play and can be dangerous. When they *do* play them, they are told to stand up and stretch out their arms, so that the cymbals sound well and the children are in no danger of the cymbal getting near to their faces. Finger cymbals are possible, but again, rather difficult for the small child to play. If used they can be introduced along with triangles. A really big cymbal which can be hung on a bar or held by an older child is really better as it's easy to play and sounds thrilling. In playing the big cymbal the child must be shown not only how to strike it, but how to stop the sound with his hand. When the older children play the smaller cymbals, they too can be shown that when they have played the cymbals they can hold them down against their bodies to "damp" or stop the sound.

When all the instruments have been introduced, and this may take several sessions, the children can divide into groups, with those playing the same instrument sitting together, and accompany a nursery rhyme. For a first group piece I usually select "I Hear Thunder", because the words make it so obvious which instruments are to play. However, there are many pieces of music as well as songs which can be scored for percussion and which the children love to play. To mention a few; "Minuet in G", Beethoven; "The Military March", Schubert; "The Lost Penny", "Beethoven; or "Donkey Riding" and "Off We Go On Our Merry-Go-Round", Canadian Folk Songs. The children can also choose any instrument they want, and "improvise" either individually, or as a group, and the teacher can join in, extemporizing* on some other instrument such as the piano or guitar.

At a later stage, we can write out a very simple score, and each child can have her own part to read. A score can be written out in pictures (see example) or notes. Every child should be given the opportunity to conduct, and when repeating a tune I not only change conductors, but if time allows, change instruments, so that each child has the opportunity of playing the instrument of her choice. It is also important to score the music that is used for group playing so that everyone comes in during the last two or three phrases. It is really difficult for small children, even if they have already played their instrument, to wait while the others play. If they know in advance that they are going to come in again at the end, waiting is not so difficult.

58

"Polly Put the Kettle On"

● Drum △ Triangle ◆ Tambourine **9** Rattle

Verse 1   Verse 2

or let the children make up their own pictures.

Making instruments should be encouraged and a child with her parents' help can easily make drums and rattles. Some parents come up with a variety of excellent home-made instruments which the children love to bring to their music class. It is also a good idea, when all the instruments have been introduced, to let the children choose the one they like best, and draw it in their books. Drawing helps the child to observe the details of the instrument, and learn its name, which we write under the drawing. It also helps *us* to discover which instrument the child likes best.

Using percussion instruments to dramatize poetry has already been discussed in the chapter on **Music and the Arts,** and this kind of dramatization can be extended into stories such as, "Noah and the Ark", "Billy Goats Gruff", or "The Night Before Christmas". Percussion instruments can also be used with great effect to represent characters in songs. For example, "There was an Old Woman Who Swallowed a Fly" (Alan Mills); "I Bought Me a Cat and the Cat Pleased Me" (Folk Song), or the carol "Jesus, Our Master Kind and Good". In fact, the number of interesting things that can be done with percussion instruments is legion; and if we run out of ideas the children are usually quite ready to suggest some new and hither to untried combination.

*"Extemporizing" means making something up as you go along, and it comes naturally to most young children who make up songs as they play, and particularly when they travel (by boat, bus or car) unless prevented by their parents who feel they are drawing attention to themselves! In our music classes we can encourage the children to make up stories; accompanied by the percussion instruments, songs; (using words they know and making up the tune, or putting new words to a well-known tune) or making up melodies on the chime bars, xylophones or piano. As they gain experience they may be able to add an *ostinato* to a song, or a few chords and as this type of musical activity teaches them to listen, it is worthwhile, as well as being most enjoyable.

I HEAR THUNDER

Words: Barbara Cass Beggs   Melody: Nursery Rhyme "Frère Jacques

THIS OLD MAN

English Folk Song

Conducting

It is difficult to classify conducting for it belongs in so many musical categories. It is part of movement, rhythm, dynamics and percussion. It also belongs in the emotional field for children find emotional release in conducting. It provides a means of self-expression and it develops a sense of self-confidence.

With beginners, you should use a very free movement with both arms swinging from the shoulder, to avoid a tight or restricted movement. A steady beat is kept but there is no need to indicate whether the music is in two, three, or four time. Gradually, as the children become more confident, they can indicate when the music is to be played loudly or softly, quickly or slowly, when it is to begin, when it is to stop. By degrees, they learn to look at, or even indicate which children are to play next, and to show where the strong beat comes. After some practice in conducting, and when they have become increasingly aware of loud and soft beats, they can learn the correct patterns for two, three, four and five time, and by listening to a variety of songs and music, they will soon be able to discover the time patterns for themselves. Later, they will find that they need to discover whether the music starts on a down or an up beat, and again, this is a skill they can acquire by listening to a number of songs or short pieces of music which begin with strong or weak beat. If they have any difficulty in hearing, or perhaps understanding the down and up beat, let them move to the music before they try conducting it.

2　　　　　**3**　　　　　**4**

Five time is a combination of two and three, or three and two.

SUGGESTIONS FOR LISTENING

Simple Time

Two Time: *Á La Claire Fontaine* (Canadian Folk Song)
  London Bridge N'R'
Three Time: *Un Canadien Errant* (Canadian Folk Song)
  Jack Be Nimble N.R.
Four Time: *Land of the Silver Birch* (Canadian Folk Song)
  Baa, Baa, Black Sheep N.R.
Five Time *Searching for Lambs* (English Folk Song) (2-3)
  The Tambourin (Spanish Folk Song) (3-2)
  The two songs in five time can be found in "Folk Songs of Europe" (See bibliography)
Compound Time: (6-8) *Oh Come, My Top, Will You Dance With Me* (Canadian Folk Song)
  Boys and Girls Come Out to Play N.R.
Up Beat: *The Ash Grove* (Traditional)
Down Beat: *Early One Morning* (Traditional)

Reading Music: Rhythm and Notation

Music is a combination of rhythm and pitch, so in order to read music, children need to know and understand musical symbols (notation) and musical intervals[1] which provide the melody.

A rhythm alone can be very dull, for example:

but add a melody and it is Beethoven's lovely, "Hymn of Joy" from the *Choral Symphony*. A melody can also be unattractive, in fact it does not make sense until a rhythmic pattern is added to it. For example C B A G F E D C does not convey anything beyond a scale, but add rhythm, and it becomes the first phrase of a Handel melody sung to the carol, *"Joy to the World".*[3]

Therefore, there are two steps which must be taken in learning to read music, getting to know the notes and their time patterns and getting to know the intervals of the scales upon which melodies are built. Both these learning processes need to go hand in hand, and both are made easy, using the Curwen time names (see notation table) accompanied by Solfége, and hand signs (see pitch table).

The reading process goes through various stages. To begin with it is easier to teach rhythm and pitch separately (for each has its own movements, patterns and songs). At a later stage, rhythm and pitch come together and it is this combination which constitutes "reading" music.

HYMN OF JOY

JOY TO THE WORLD

---

[1] An interval is the distance in pitch between two notes. Intervals are reckoned from the lowest note which is called one.

Stage One (Rhythm and Notation)

At first children need to have lots of fun with rhythmic patterns before bothering about actual notation. In moving to the drum they walk, skip, jump, run, gallop, and each of these movements has a different rhythmic pattern. We can ask children questions, which they can answer rhythmically (clapping, on the drum, or rhythm sticks) such as "What is your name?", "What colour are your socks?" This presents them with a variety of rhythmic patterns.

(Walk) ♩♩♩♩ (Skip) ♩♪♩♪ (Run) ♫♫♫♫ (Jump) ♩♩♩ (Gallop) ♫♩♫♩

♩♫♩ (What is your name?) ♩♩♫♩ (What colour are your socks?)

♩ (Pink)   ♩♩ (Daisy)   ♫ (Buttercup)   ♩ (Rose)

After a few sessions of moving rhythmically and answering rhythmic questions you can show them pictures of three clocks. A grandfather clock, which says, "tick-tock"   ♩♩   very slowly, a kitchen clock, which says, "tick-tock, tick-tock" ♩♩♩♩   more quickly, and a little watch which says, "tick-tock, tick-tock, tick-tock"   ♫♫♫♫   very quickly. The children can play the clock rhythms on the rhythm sticks and it is fun to follow these rhythms with the singing of "Hickory Dickory Dock". (I like to accompany this nursery rhyme, and when we come to the line, "the mouse ran down", the children can slide their sticks down while I make a big "glissando"[4] on the piano)

At the close of a rhythm stick session, children can put the sticks away to the melody of "Books Away", or they can pretend that they are candles, flags, or trays, or anything else that they suggest, and march around with them to quiet music before putting them away. I find that they love "pretence candles", which they light with great care and "blow out" before dropping them in a box or bag.

Another way of listening to the pulse or pattern, (or time and rhythm) is to tell them that when the doctor comes to see them he feels their pulse in order to see whether they are well or not. If their pulse is slow then he may suggest that they are tired. If their pulse is quick, then they may have a fever. If their pulse moves evenly and happily, then they are quite well. I ask them to find the pulse in their wrist and we play the three types of pulse that I have mentioned on the rhythm sticks. ♩ ♩ ♫

By this time they can begin to play the rhythmic patterns of nursery rhymes, and children who are three or four, (the twos find this too difficult), can divide into two groups, with one group playing the pulse and the other the pattern. For example:

Pattern   pulse
(Mary Had a Little Lamb)   ♩♫♫♩♩   ♩♩♩♩

When the children are not playing the rhythm sticks or there is a short break in the rhythmic pattern place the sticks on either side of the child, or have them hold the sticks up in the air. In both these positions the sticks are ready for playing but not where the child will be tempted to continue to hit them.

[4] See musical terms in the appendix.

Stage Two (Rhythm and Notation)

This is a most enjoyable stage for children, because they are introduced to what I call "The Musical Family", and the children learn them very quickly because they love the idea of the family.

Not more than two notes are introduced at a time, and I start off with *Ta* or "Big Brother" (♩) who marches, and *Ta-a* or "Mother" (♩) who walks more slowly as she is probably carrying a heavy shopping bag or wheeling a stroller. *Ta* goes "step, step" *Ta-a* goes "step-pause, step-pause" and we wave our arms on the pause because this makes it easier to balance. Next come the "Twins" *Ti-Ti* (♫) *who run and also hold hands and "Grand-father" Ta-a-a-a( ) who walks very slowly. Before introducing "The Triplets" Ti-Ti-Ti ( ) and the "Quadruplets" Ta-fa-te-fe ( ) who run very quickly, we discuss what we call "babies" who are born two at a time, three at a time or four at a time (a most unusual event!) so the children are ready for the new names. As they meet and move to each member of the family they also play them on the rhythm sticks or the drum and draw them in their books.*

THE MUSICAL FAMILY

𝅝 Whole note (Grandfather) Ta-a-a-a   Barbara Cass Beggs

Twelfth note (Triplet) Ti-ti-ti — Jesu Joy. J.S Bach

Sixteenth Note (Quadruplet) Ta-fa-té-fé — Barbara Cass Beggs

I am run-ning, I am run-ning, I am run-ning ve-ry fast.

I am run-ning, I am run-ning, you can catch me at the last.

Once they are familiar with the **musical family** all kinds of games can be played. Pictures of them can be scattered around the room and the children can find which one I am playing (on the drum or on the piano). They can play "Snap" with a collection of their pictures. They can try to build a tune, such as "Polly Put the Kettle On" from a collection of notes piled up in any order. You can give each child a pile of notes which will make up a melody, and ask them to "unscramble" them. We clap the melodies first so that they know how their melody sounds. At this stage the children often bring me pictures which they have made at home of the **musical family,** and they like to play their pictures on the drum or on the piano.

During a drum and rhythm-stick session, the rhythmic patterns of animals, flowers, colours, trees, names or food can be played or sung to the musical family names. Bluebell (♩♩) Rose (♩) Dandelion (♪♪♪) etc., and one can begin to join these patterns up, for example Pine (♩) Oak (♩) Holly (♫) Christmas Tree (♫♩) with the musical symbols written underneath the picture, or a big card with a variety of rhythmic patterns written on it. The children can then clap the note symbols and sing the musical family names. Nursery rhymes or short poems can be written out and played on the rhythm sticks, and it is possible to include a brief rhythmic *ostinato* such as one child playing "buns, buns, buns" (♪♪♪) while the others play the rhythm of

Hot Cross Buns (♪♪♩ ♪♪♩ ♪♪♪♪♪♪ ♪♪♩)

When the children are happy with easy rhythmic patterns using the **musical family** they can understand that "silences" (rests) are just as important as sounds. We play our sticks, hitting them together to make a loud sound, and then hitting them in the air to make *no* sound. I ask them to listen to this "silence" and suggest that no sound at all is rather pleasant. From an appreciation of silence we move to the introduction of the *rests,* which at first I call "chairs" on which the **musical family** sit when they are not singing. We look at their pictures and discover using the time names, that when grandfather rests, he whispers "Sa-a-a-a". We then play a kind of musical chairs which involves moving when the family moves and sitting on the floor when the family rests or sits on a chair (and we whisper their names using *s* instead of *t*). This makes a very exciting game,* particularly when we come to the twins and the triplets, for everyone is constantly up and down on the floor! Finally, having experienced all the rests, the children draw them in their books. In future classes they can be included in their rhythmic patterns and on their picture cards which we put out for the children to guess. Although they will not remember all of them, they will remember the ones we use most, and more importantly, they will have been made aware that musical silences are important and have their own symbols.

Rests

Sa-a-a-a   Sa-a   Sa   si-si-   si-si-si-   sa-fa-se-fe

Stage Three (Rhythm and Notation)

Naturally, as the children progress, they come across more complicated rhythms, such as the tied or dotted note. I find it helps if I suggest that if "Mother" (𝅗𝅥) holds on to "Big Brother" (𝅘𝅥) so (𝅗𝅥 𝅘𝅥) "Big Brother" has to remain silent, and "Mother" adds an extra *a* to her voice (𝅗𝅥 𝅘𝅥 *ta-a-a).* I also suggest that a quick way of writing this is to put a dot instead of a note so that you get (𝅗𝅥.). Many examples can be illustrated 𝅝 𝅘𝅥 𝅝 𝅗𝅥𝅗𝅥 𝅗𝅥. 𝅘𝅥𝅘𝅥 𝅘𝅥.

and because most of the children are aware of wholes and halves by now, (a whole apple, a half apple), they can understand that a dot following a note equals half the note which proceeds it.

Syncopation provides another complicated rhythm, although children can play a syncopated beat quite easily before they realize what it is. If they learn, "'My Paddle Keen and Bright" and "Land of the Silver Birch", both appealing songs, they can sing and then play on the rhythm sticks the syncopated bars in these songs, and we can point out that the reason they sound "different" is because we usually accent the first beat in any song or piece of music and here the accent comes on the second beat.

"Potato" (𝅘𝅥𝅮𝅘𝅥𝅘𝅥𝅮) provides another good example of the syncopated beat, and one can write out the names of four vegetables, ask the children to put the correct notation under the names and find which is the syncopated vegetable.

Pea 𝅘𝅥 Carrot 𝅘𝅥𝅮𝅘𝅥𝅮 Potatoe 𝅘𝅥𝅮𝅘𝅥𝅘𝅥𝅮 Beetroot 𝅘𝅥𝅘𝅥

They can also clap or drum *Syn-co-pa* (𝅘𝅥𝅮𝅘𝅥𝅘𝅥𝅮) and learn the word *Syncopation.* In order to discover how alert they are in observing which notation represents which rhythm, put out six cards with different rhythmic patterns on each, including a syncopated one, play one at a time and ask the children, in turn to pick up the correct card.

It is possible at this stage to play a rhythmic question and expect a rhythmic or balancing answer, for example, question: (𝅘𝅥 𝅘𝅥𝅮𝅘𝅥𝅮 𝅘𝅥 𝅘𝅥) answer: (𝅘𝅥𝅮𝅘𝅥𝅮 𝅘𝅥𝅮𝅘𝅥𝅮 𝅘𝅥). We might also expect, that with a little encouragement some of the children will begin to make up songs, particularly if we start them off, for example: "My Pussy Cat" (𝅘𝅥 𝅘𝅥𝅮𝅘𝅥𝅮 𝅘𝅥), "She is very fat . . ." (𝅘𝅥𝅮𝅘𝅥𝅮 𝅘𝅥𝅮𝅘𝅥𝅮 𝅘𝅥) Before expecting children to rhyme, it's a good idea to have a session on rhyming words. What rhymes with "cat"? hot? sit? my? Children love making up silly rhymes and a nonsense rhyme like "Wibbley wobbleby woo, an elephant sat on me/Wibbley wobbelby wam, an elephant sat in the jam!" helps everyone to make up rhymes — even if they are silly!

You don't need to embark on an explanation of simple (every note divides into two beats) time, once the children have met the dotted note they might be encouraged to look at and walk and skip to 6/8 patterns. (𝅗𝅥.𝅗𝅥.|𝅗𝅥. or 𝅘𝅥𝅮𝅘𝅥𝅮𝅘𝅥𝅮|𝅘𝅥𝅮𝅘𝅥𝅮𝅘𝅥𝅮|𝅘𝅥𝅮𝅘𝅥𝅮𝅘𝅥𝅮)When they try to conduct a song in 6/8 time, they will discover that 6/8 is compound duple and it is better to conduct with two beats, not six. As they are unlikely to meet 9/8 or 12/8 compound time, these are not introduced here. (If needed they can be introduced in the same way as 6/8 time.)

CANOE SONG (ROUND) Canadian Folk Song

(1) My pad- dle's keen and bright (2) flash-ing with sil-ver.

(3) Follow the wild goose flight, (4) dip-dip and swing.

LAND OF THE SILVER BIRCH Canadian Folk Song

Land of the sil- ver birch, home of the bea- ver

where still the migh-ty moose wan-ders at will.

Blue lake and rock- y shore, I will re- turn once more

Boom did-dy boom boom boom did-dy boom boom boom. did-dy boom boom boom.

Xylophone or chime bars through-out Drum (etc) at end to follow song pattern.

o whole	≡	half	≡	quarter	¿
Ta-a-a-a	Sa-a-a-a	Ta-a	Sa-a	Ta	Sa

eighth ɣɣ   twelfth ɣɣɣ   sixteenth ɣɣɣɣ

Ti-Ti Si-si   Ti-ti-ti si si si   ta-fa-te-fe Sa-fa-se-fe

Combinations:

Tied and Dotted Notes:

The *Curwen* time names were adapted from the Galin-Paris Chève method. Since then they have been used and modified by various people including Kodály, who changed (♫) *ta-té* to *ti-ti*, which is better as it avoids confusion with *ta*. (He also uses *tri-o-la* for the triplets and keeps *ti-ti-ti* for the compound 6/8 rhythm of (♫♪).

I keep to the *ti-ti-ti* for the triplet and the Curwen tafa-téfé. (Kodály uses *ti-ri-ti-ri*). It is unimportant which sounds are used as long as they are used consistently and accurately represent the time length of the note.

Notes 1-3 are pronounced "AR."; for the sixteenth note ta-fa-te-fe" "a" is pronounced as in apple.

Table of Times Names (Curwen)

SIMPLE TIME: (Beats divided into two)

Duple	$\frac{2}{2}$	$\frac{2}{4}$	$\frac{2}{8}$	or	2♩ 2♩ 2♪
Triple	$\frac{3}{2}$	$\frac{3}{4}$	$\frac{3}{8}$	or	3♩ 3♩ 3♪
Quadruple	$\frac{4}{2}$	$\frac{4}{4}$	$\frac{4}{8}$	or	4♩ 4♩ 4♪

COMPOUND TIME (Beats divide into three)

Compound Duple	$\frac{6}{4}$	$\frac{6}{8}$	$\frac{6}{16}$	or	$\frac{2}{\text{♩.}}$	$\frac{2}{\text{♩.}}$	$\frac{2}{\text{♪.}}$	
Compound Triple	$\frac{9}{4}$	$\frac{9}{8}$	$\frac{9}{16}$	or	$\frac{3}{\text{♩.}}$	$\frac{3}{\text{♩.}}$	$\frac{3}{\text{♪.}}$	
Compound Quadruple	$\frac{12}{4}$	$\frac{12}{8}$	$\frac{12}{16}$	or	$\frac{4}{\text{♩.}}$	$\frac{4}{\text{♩.}}$	$\frac{4}{\text{♪.}}$	

Reading Music, Melody, Pitch and Solfége

STAGE ONE

Pitch games are very useful in developing your child's ability to hear and reproduce sounds of varying pitch and can be introduced in a variety of ways and at a variety of times.

I usually start with the Ball or Balloon songs. I give each child, a pretence ball or pretence balloon, and sing the song with the appropriate actions, (this usually involves singing it twice, as we recapture our balloons and balls). We sing top *doh,* bottom *doh* and *soh,* making the appropriate hand signs. Each child is then given three coloured paper balls or balloons to put in her book and beside these I write the three sounds *D, D,¹ & S,* getting each child to repeat the hand movements as I write the names. I do not explain what we are doing, we just sing, move and "stick" the three sounds in their books. They can also add a coloured string to their balloon if they wish.

BALLOONS / KITES

Barbara Cass-Beggs

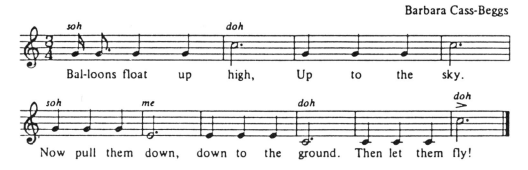

(Jump in the air on "fly!")
Instead of balloons, kites can be used.

At the next class, I tell them the story of the Three Bears. We listen to their high, low and medium voices and then play at *being* bears. Walking on tip-toe for Baby Bear, walking with arms folded for Mother Bear, and crawling for Father Bear. The children then listen while I play the "Bear Music" and move according to which bear is being played. I then suggest that they come and find the bear's voices themselves on the piano. The song "Jack-in-a-Box" provides another variation on the Bear Games because they have to listen in order to find out whether the music is high, low or in the middle and then they move accordingly.

Another way of introducing the three *Sol-Fa* sounds is to tell a story using a glockenspiel or xylophone. I tell them a story about a little boy who lives at the bottom of a hill in a house named *Doh,* who goes to visit his little friend who lives in a house at the top of the hill, called *Doh*. On the way up, he gets very tired and stops to visit with another little friend, who lives in a house which is about half way up the hill, and his house is called *Soh*. When he has rested, he hurries on to the house at the top, (and I wait for the children to tell me its name), and then he runs all the way home to his own house at the bottom of the hill, which is called? (Doh!). We sing these houses with the hand movements, and I then ask the children to close their eyes and guess which house I am playing. Having done this they can try to find and play the three sounds (or houses) themselves, and try to make their own voices sing high, low and middle sounds.

If the musical signals have been used, the children are already familiar with the intervals of *Soh-Doh* (a 5th) (sit down), and *Soh-Doh* (a 4th) (stand up). They have also heard the interval of *Soh-Me* (a minor 3rd) not only in our song, "Books Away", but also in many nursery rhymes and singing games. Therefore, I introduce the *Soh-Me* interval next. It is a very natural interval for calling someone, *Ma-ry, (Soh-Me)* and we can now begin each class by asking each child to sing her name. "What is your name *S S S M?"* (♫♩), *Ma-ry (S-M)* (♫). Another good way of introducing this interval is to give the children a variety of bells to play. We sing the Bell Song, and then put two paper bells in our books saying *Soh-Me* (Ding-Dong) (♩♩).

TWINKLE TWINKLE LITTLE STAR

Idea - Barbara Cass-Beggs   Nursery Rhyme

* Another fun song to sing, using two lines is "Space Ships" by Grace Nash.

Before learning any more new Sol-Fa intervals there are a number of other pitch games which the children enjoy. In one, the percussion instruments represent high, low and middle sounds (bells, tambourines, drums). I play them where the children cannot see them, and they have to move according to which instrument is played. We can also pretend that we are cleaning a house which involves sweeping the cobwebs off the ceiling (high music), polishing the table (middle music), and scrubbing the floor (low music). A story can be told about a stormy day, rain (bells), heavy rain (tambourines), and thunder (drums), which can again represent the three Sol-Fa sounds. If there is a group of somewhat older children (5-6), we can sing some well-known nursery rhymes and see if they can put in the *Doh* at the end. "One for the little boy who lived down the lane?" (Doh), or you can ask the children to go for a walk and run home (we mark a spot for home), when they hear the home sound *Doh*.

BALLS / STRETCH

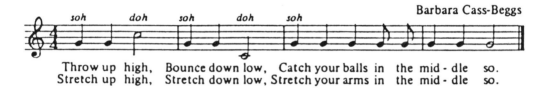

Barbara Cass-Beggs

Throw up high, Bounce down low, Catch your balls in the mid-dle so.
Stretch up high, Stretch down low, Stretch your arms in the mid-dle so.

Any number of different word versions can be made up.

BELL SONG   Barbara Cass Beggs

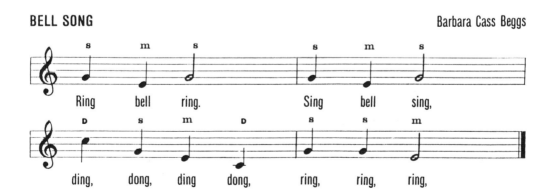

Ring   bell   ring.   Sing   bell   sing,

ding,   dong,   ding   dong,   ring,   ring,   ring,

JACK-IN-A-BOX

Children pretend to be jack-in-a-boxes. When they spring out they move according to the pitch of the music which is played. (Like the three bears.)

STAGE TWO

Because from now on we will be using the chime bars, I produce four chime bars, *Doh, Me, Soh* and top *Doh,* and we practice using the hammer freely and comfortably, hitting the bar in the middle and stopping its vibrations by putting their hands on the chime bar when they have played, for it not only stops the sound, but stops the children from continuing to play. I also suggest that each child hold the chime bar up to her ear, when she has struck it, so that she can hear the musical vibrations. We are now ready to find the children's names on *Soh* and *Me,* and find and play the two *Dohs.* It is also enjoyable to play the four sounds together so that the children can hear the effect of a "chord"[1]

As I work with very young children I find it helpful to use colours for the different notes of the scale, and I have adopted the colours used by Dr. Mary Helen Richards[2]. Black for *Doh,* Green for *Ray,* Blue for *Me,* Orange for *Fah,* Red for *Soh,* Yellow for *Lah,* Brown for *Te,* and Black again for top *Doh.* Chime bars can be coloured with crayons or coloured paper stuck on, and when the children reach the stage of song patterns (notation) and their accompanying Sol-Fa sounds, these too can be coloured. Although I do not want to stress the colours, for children should recognize sounds through listening to them, not by looking at their colour, it does help the twos and threes to find the Sol-Fa sounds more easily.[3]

Our next step will be to combine the musical family notation with the Sol-Fa, so we learn the song "Daffodil". First, each child chooses a flower and we "grow up" to the various flowers as we sing the song. Then we clap the melody, sing the correct musical family names, and try to play it on the chime bars. Because it is hard to play. I suggest that half the class sing and play the hand signs, and the other half play the chime bars. It is also possible to divide the song up, so that some children play the part where *Doh* comes in and the others play the *Soh-Me* part. (Incidentally, when using the hand signs I use both hands, to avoid the confusion of right and left and the mirror image.)

DAFFODIL

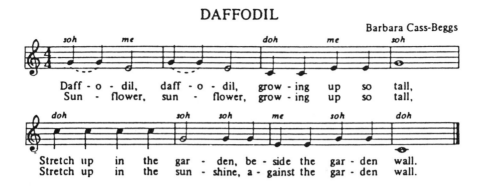

Barbara Cass-Beggs

| soh | me | | doh | me | soh |

Daff - o - dil, daff - o - dil, grow - ing up so tall,
Sun - flower, sun - flower, grow - ing up so tall,

| doh | soh | soh | me | soh | doh |

Stretch up in the gar - den, be - side the gar - den wall.
Stretch up in the sun - shine, a - gainst the gar - den wall.

Lah is introduced next because it is such a natural sound to sing, and it occurs in so many nursery rhymes. The children watch and imitate the new hand sign, find it in "Ring Around a Rosy", or "Bye Baby Bunting", and then see if they can play a song containing the new sound on the chime bars. "Bell Horses" is a good song to choose because the children can sing it first in a question and answer form using the percussion instruments (bells and rhythm sticks). Then they can clap it, singing the musical family names, find *Lah* on the chime bars, and finally play the song on the chime bars.

[1] A chord means playing two or more notes at the same time.
[2] Dr. Mary Helen Richards of *The Richards Institute of Music Education & Research,* U.S.A.
[3] Candida Tobin has introduces another approach to colour which she uses to identify notes and musical theory. Each scale is a different colour and instruments are taught using colour charts.

BELL HORSES

(Lah)

N.R.

Bell hor-ses bell hor-ses what's the time of day?

One o'- clock two o'- clock No time to stay.

BYE BABY BUNTING
(Lah)

(Lullaby) N.R.

By ba-by bunt-ing dad-dy's gone a- hunt-ing, to get a lit-tle

rab-bit skin, to wrap a ba-by bunt-ing in. By ba-by bunt- ing

The introduction of *Ray* completes the *Pentatonic** or five note scale, and the nursery rhyme, "Rain is falling Down" provides an excellent introduction to *Ray*, with the added advantage that it also introduces a rest in the time pattern. Again, it is fun to sing the song first, using the percussion instruments. Bells for the first two lines, triangles for the pitter-patter, and a cymbal for the "splash" which represents the rest. It is a very easy melody and having clapped it and sung it to the musical family notation they can play it on the chime bars substituting a "sa" (in the air) for the rest instead of the cymbal.

* In his work with young children, Kodály concentrated on the pentatonic scale and this is not surprising as he was basing his teaching on Hungarian folk songs, and Hungarian folk music is basically Pentatonic. He also kept to the Pentatonic scale because he thought that young children found it difficult to sing semitones in tune. In my baby classes, I have found that the babies often sing in semitones and I noted that my grandson when lying in his cot sang   C B Bb A Ab G,   over and over again — to a kind of la-ing sound and perfectly in pitch. I have also found that twos and threes, in my music classes, seem to have no special difficulty with semitones. Perhaps this points to the fact that children absorb the sound patterns of their cultural background and this suggests that different cultural backgrounds not only provide great variation but certainly need to be taken into account when we come to teach music to young children.

RAIN IS FALLING DOWN
(Ray)

N.R.

Rain is fall-ing down. Splash! Rain is fall-ing down. Splash!

Pit-ter pat-ter pit-ter pat-ter Rain is fall-ing down. Splash!

Before we start stage two I draw a picture of eight chime bars in the children's books and then each time we learn a Sol-Fa sound we colour in the appropriate chime bar. They enjoy doing this and it makes it possible for them to sing the songs that they have played on the chime bars, from their books, putting their fingers on each picture chime bar as they sing it, and this of course, encourages *pre-hearing* the sounds, which is an essential for all sight reading. I also write out the songs they are going to play, with the rhythmic pattern and Sol-Fa signs (in colour) so that when they clap the rhythm they can also look at it.

Stage Three (5-6 years)

Songs based on the Pentatonic scale are very easy to sing, and almost any combination of these notes sounds pleasant. Although the word Pentatonic can be applied to any five note melody, it is usually applied to the gapped scale *C D E G A*, which can be found by playing the black notes on the piano. The children enjoy finding this scale on the black notes and it is interesting for them to know that Chinese music and before that, Babylonian music, was based on this scale, so it is a very early scale. Because of its Chinese connection it is fun to bring along a willow-pattern plate, tell them the story associated with the plate, and then play on the black notes "Willow Pattern Plates We Like to See" **C♯ D♯ F♯ G♯ A♯** "Willow Pattern Plates are Fun for Tea". (Play up and down twice).

Having now discovered the black notes we can look at drawings of *sharps* and *flats*, and the children can be shown that although these do not always occur on the black notes (show them **E**) **A♯** or ♭ always makes a note one-half step or semitone higher or lower. E.g. **C-C♯, or B-B♭**

If the children are still interested in the black notes and semitones they can listen to, play or walk to the Chromatic Scale[4], making up words to it if they like. For example: "We take every little step and they are very small (up). We walk rather like the way a slimy snake would crawl" (down).

Because the majority of North American and British songs are "diatonic"[5] (although some are modal[6]) this scale can now be introduced. Again pitch games such as "Up the Ladder", or "One Little Snowman" are useful and the children can learn *sol-fa* signs for *Te* and *Fah*, and colour them in their books, pointing out that *Te* nearly always goes up to *Doh* (hence the up-pointing finger) and *Fah* nearly always drops down to *Me* (hence the down-pointing thumb).

UP THE LADDER

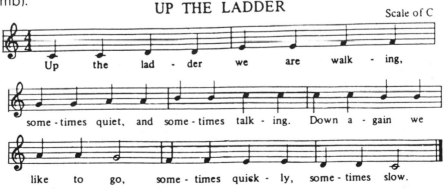

Scale of C

The children walk up the ladder, coming down backwards. Try to take one step to each note (or rung).

ONE LITTLE SNOWMAN
(TEDDY BEAR, TULIP)

This song can be sung, and the children stand up one by one. It can be played on the chime bars — or glockenspiel. It can be found on the piano.

When the children know the whole scale they can have fun suggesting different words for different intervals. For example *Soh-Doh* can say, "Hee-Haw", *Te-Doh* "At Home", *Me-Ray-Doh* "Lullaby". One of the children suggested that a glissando from *Doh* to *Doh* could say "Skating" and another that *Soh-Doh* could say "Hurray!". You can test the children's ability to recognize the different tones of the scale by asking them to play whatever sounds you play on the chime bars. At first they can watch what you play, then see if they can imitate what you play without looking. Three, four or five notes are enough to begin with, and when they can imitate these sounds quite easily you can try playing the beginning of a song that they know, for example, the first phrase of "Teddy Bear" or "I have a dog". First get them to clap the rhythm, and tell you whether the melody is in two, three or four time. It is always fun to finish a chime bar session, once they know the diatonic scale, by singing and playing, "I Have a Little Pussy".

I HAVE A DOG
(Ray)

N.R.

[4] A chromatic scales moves in semitones which use the same letter name, i.e., C C♯, D D♯. The word *chromatic* comes from the Greek work "Chroma" (colour).

[5] A seven-note scale with its octave is called "diatonic" from the Greek word meaning "through the notes". The steps in the scale vary in size and this gives the scale its particular shape or melody.

[6] Modal scales begin on *C D E F G A*. The semi-tones vary with each scale. The modes are called Ionian, Dorian, and Phryian, Lydian, Mixo-Lydian and Aeolian. The Ionian mode of *C* is known as the scale of *C major,* owing to the position of its semi-tones, it is a diatonic scale.

Before introducing the *great staff* (see stage five) children can begin to read the *Sol-Fa* sounds with the time names on two lines, for this gets them started on reading (from the lines and spaces) and helps their eyes to follow a line that moves from left to right, and also moves up and down. You can start with very simple words like their names and then move on to a short song such as "The Moon"*

Ma-ry Jon-a-than   Zoom Zoom Zoom, Let's go to the moon, Zoom-off

I CAN SING UP HIGH

Idea - Diller-Page

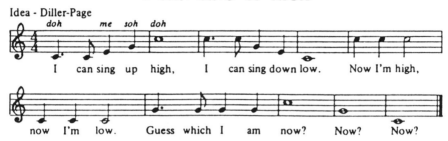

Pitch table

Doh (Do)

Ray (Re)

Me (Mi)

Fah (Fa)

Soh (So)

Lah (La)

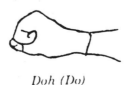

Doh (Do)

TEDDY BEAR N.R.
(Ray & Lah)

Ted-dy bear,   Ted-dy bear turn a- round,   Ted-dy bear Ted-dy bear, touch the ground

Ted-dy bear,   Ted-dy bear   show your shoe,   Ted-dy bear, Ted-dy bear,   that will do.

By this time the children shouls be aware that *Doh* moves, so they should be able to read their names in different positions (keys) and practice singing a well-known melody such as "Three Blind Mice" with the hand signs. Changing the *Doh* when you change the *Doh* — for example

M-R-D, M-R-D, M-R-D, S-F-M, S-F-M.

E-D-C, E-D-C, E-D-C, G-F-E, G-F-E.

Soh now becomes *Doh* **M-R-D, M-R-D, M-R-D, S-F-M, S-F-M.**
B-A-G, B-A-G, B-A-G, D-C-B, D-C-B.

Then *Fah* can become *Doh* so that you have:-

M-R-D, M-R-D, M-R-D, S-F-M, S-F-M
A-G-F, A-G-F, A-G-F, C-B♭-A, C-B♭-A.

This is one of the joys of using the solfége system: it makes transposition (changing into another key) so much easier!

Because the melody aspect of reading included the use of the melodic instruments, here are pictures of them.

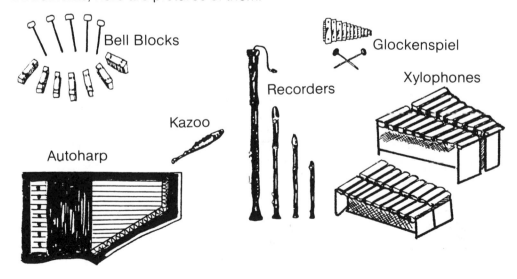

Bell Blocks

Glockenspiel

Xylophones

Recorders

Kazoo

Autoharp

CHAPTER 9

Reading, Music: Rhythm, Notation, Melody, Pitch and Solfége Together

The final Stage (5-6 Years)

Now that the children can read simple melodies using rhythmic notation and *Sol-Fa*, and have been shown what these melodies look like when written on two lines, it is time to introduce them to the *great staff*. Before actually trying to read from the staff, I tell them a story about the staff and how music came to be written, for I find children learn much more quickly when they understand the logical development of a new skill.

I explain that when people first wanted to write music they thought of using a big ladder (and I draw the *great staff* without separating the three staves), which the children are not surprised to hear was considered a little cumbersome! I go on to say that as people realized that some voices were high, (girls and mothers), some low, (men and fathers) and some in the middle, (children and some girls with low voices); this big staff was divided up into three parts, one for each voice (and I draw three five-line staves).

Having solved the problem of size, people were still uncertain about which line represented which sound. I then ask the children what keys are for and I get a variety of answers "to lock doors, to open chests, to wind clocks", etc. I tell them that it was through a key that the sound and line problem was solved, for it was decided to have a key or "clef" (which is French for key) which could be put on a certain line and would say what sound that line represented. The *G clef*, was chosen for high voices, (*G* happens to stand for *g*irls so it is easy to remember). The *F clef* was chosen for the low voices (and this is easy to remember because it stands for *f*ather), and a *C clef* was chosen for voices in the middle (and *C* stands for *c*hildren). I then put those letters in their correct places on the three staves.

Then we talk about reading, discuss the letters of the alphabet, and how they are used to make words and spell their names. We see if we can say the whole alphabet and agree if people wanted to use letter names for their music it would be very difficult if they used the whole alphabet. Actually, when music was first written only four letters of the alphabet were used and later, another three were added so finally we have *A B C D E F G*. Then we look at some old manuscripts and see how the number of lines vary, what funny notes and clefs were used and what beautiful colouring and pictures ornamented some of the music. Finally, we look at some present day music and discover that the original letters of G F and C have been changed almost beyond recognition!

Next we make a big staff on the floor with strips of paper or coloured string, using thumb tacks or books to hold it down. We make the lines wide enough so that they can walk on the lines and in the spaces. The actual walking is very important, for otherwise children find it impossible to realize that notes go *in* the spaces as well as on the lines. We then position a *G clef* and letter names (previously cut out) and the children take turns walking from *middle C* to the space at the top of the stave which is *G*. Everyone wants a turn and at the end, we roll up the staff and collect the notes which is almost as much fun as making it! I then give out manuscript paper and see if they can draw the three clefs in the right place (as they used to be: *G F C*, or as they are now). They can then write their own name, having clapped its rhythmic pattern so that they know how many notes to use, on each clef line. I point out that nowadays, we do not use the *C clef* very much, but we used to use it for alto and tenor voices, and for some of the Brass instruments. It is still useful, in that if you see a *C clef*, you will know that it represents the *C* which is approximately in the middle of the piano, and we all go and find *Middle C* on the piano!

It is helpful for the children to realize that by counting on their fingers there are seven alphabet sounds and seven *Sol-Fa* sounds and both repeat the first one, *A* or *Doh*. Our next step is to write on the blackboard (or felt board) a very easy tune that they know, because at this stage it is most important to convince them that they can read from the staff and that it is quite easy! If you select "Bell Hoses". *Soh* can be *G* and if they sing it first to *Sol-Fa*, then say the letters of the alphabet backwards, (C B A G F E D C), they will find the actual reading of the melody quite easy. I colour the notes to correspond with the *Sol-Fa* colours. Ask the children where the strong beat comes in "Bell Horses", and clap it and put accents (>) over the top of the notes, (discovering that it says **one** two). I then show them that a line, called a *bar line*, can be drawn in front of the accent which will show which note is accented, and that the distance between one bar line and another bar is called a *measure*. We then read another easy melody, this time starting on another note and from now on a little sight-reading from the staff can accompany each class.

If we look at some printed music, (the children love to look at nursery rhymes, and find the musical family, the clefs and the bar lines), we find that it says at the beginning, by the clef, whether the music is singing in twos, threes or fours, (this is called a *time signature*). We are also shown in advance whether we will have to play any *sharps* or *flats* in the melody, for they too are written in front of the clef and before the beginning of the music (and this is called a *key signature*).

When the children come to look at printed music they discover, rather to their horror, that some of the notes go *off* the staff both at the top and the bottom. I agree this is confusing, but the staff is limited and these notes have to make their own lines, which are called *léger* (French for *light*) lines, and need to be specially drawn for the very high and very low notes.

Both parents and children are very excited when the children show them their work books with "real" music in them, and I usually see that the card they take home at the last class contains a short melody written on the staff.

Naturally, this is only a beginning, but it is an exciting beginning, and some children pick up reading very quickly, while others are less interested and find it more difficult.

At this time the class might be divided into two groups and given fifteen minutes of recorder and fifteen minutes of piano. Not a great deal is learned in such a short period, but it gives the children an idea of a blowing instrument and of the piano, and it certainly helps their sight reading. It also puts them in a better position to move on to some other teacher and learn to play the instrument of their choice. When the group comes together again for the remaining half hour, time can be given to songs, dances, percussion, dramatizations, and many things that previously we have had difficulty in squeezing in!

The joy of teaching this final year with the children is because of their increasing ability to listen, so that we do not waste any time, and their delighted responsiveness to any new musical "happenings"!

EASY MELODY   We start our reading in the key of C and gradually move to G and F.

Enriching a child's life through music

We now come to the most exciting and colourful aspects of music, often omitted in the musical training of young children: **expression**, which defines the manner in which music is played (happily, sadly, smoothly, abruptly, sweetly, fiercely, rapidly, or slowly), and **dynamics**, which defines the gradation of loudness and softness in the musical tones. Both expression and dynamics provide an enrichment which is an essential part of music, and if children are not aware of this enrichment they miss half the joy of listening to music. Expression and dynamics remain somewhat intangible aspects because they depend on those who conduct, perform or interpret the music for their final definition. However, they also provide exciting differences, differences which especially appeal to a child's imagination.

One way in which children can become aware of the variety of musical enrichments is through the world of sounds, for long before children are aware of music as music, they are aware of a variety of sounds. In a music session, children can be asked to make or describe some of the sounds that they have heard on their way to music class: a school bus, a car hooting, the stamping of boots, a dripping tap, a doorbell ringing, or a door banging, a dog barking, people talking, or sounds that they have heard at home (the lawn mower, a typewriter, etc). they can try to make these sounds, first individually, and then together. Once they have made and thought about these sounds, ask them to find objects in the room which will make interesting sounds, not limiting it to musical instruments. Children are surprisingly inventive, and they will come up with all kinds of sounds which adults are not aware of, for example; tapping the glass of the window, banging a variety of blocks together, setting a shell mobile in motion, closing a big book, tapping a pencil on the floor, smacking their tummy. Children should have played all the kitchen instruments and perhaps other household items when they were babies, (if not they should be able to play them now!), so this sound session should form an extension of earlier experience.

In order to train their listening ability, get the children to close their eyes while you hit or tap various items in the room. They should be able to name the item and say which part of the room the sound is coming from. They can then take turns in tapping various objects, and getting their companions to guess where and what they are. Sound can be reflected from hard surfaces, and the reflection is called an echo. Children can be asked to listen to the echo of their voices when they are under a bridge, in a tunnel or in a narrow passage with walls on either side.

At the next sound session, we can go a step further and ask them to discover which sounds make a high or low sound; a loud or soft sound; a pleasant or unpleasant sound; which sounds are difficult to imitate, which easy? They can be asked to make the kind of sounds that they would hear if they were walking in a wood: the rustle of leaves, the creak of the branches, a bird singing, the chatter of a squirrel, the crack of a twig, a nut falling; or listening to the sounds made by the wind when it blows in the trees, bangs the gate shut, blows the lid off the garbage pail, and sends leaves and paper flying up into the air. These sounds can be imitated on the percussion instruments or anything else in the room which the children think is appropriate.

Another interesting sound experiment could be the creation of a storm. A slow drip-drop can be played on the chime bars followed by the quick pitter-patter of the triangles which can be joined by the bells, and as the rain increases, by the rattles. The boom of the drum and the clash of the cymbals can represent thunder and lightning, and the storm which could begin quietly, can build up to a climax, and gradually die away. It is possible and even more exciting to include other musical sounds such as the piano, the auto-harp or a gong, if these are available.

At this stage, they will be ready to listen to a simple drum roll, such as the one that comes at the beginning of Sibelius' "Finlandia", and you can ask them to describe the drum roll with their bodies in any way they like. I have found that a variety of interpretations follow. Some of the children pretend to play the drum, others become seeds or bulbs pushing up through the earth, some think it more like the taking off of a jet plane. Another time, you can give them rhythm sticks and let them "play", while listening to Orffs' "Crescendo[1]", a marvelous piece of music which begins very softly and gets louder and louder. When they have listened and played, they can be told that this gradual increase in volume and intensity which they have enjoyed so much, has a special name, "crescendo", which they can make with their arms (start with both hands on the chest and then stretch out the arms to their fullest extent in the shape of a V or crescendo) and then draw it in their books. They can then listen to music which starts loudly and gets softer, for example the opening of the slow movement of Beethoven's "Fifth Symphony", where the melody begins fairly loudly with the strings and is echoed very softly by the woodwind. They can then make a *diminuendo* with their arms (the reverse of the crescendo) and again draw its picture in their books. Finally, we make crescendos and diminuendos with our arms, at the same time, saying the names. Getting as loud as possible for the crescendos and starting loud but getting as soft as possible for the diminuendo. In making these movements, we should be aware that a crescendo grows in intensity as well as loudness, just as the diminuendo is accompanied by relaxation and a change in muscular tension.

A sense of climax is experienced by gradation of tone, but it can also be experienced rhythmically, as in Brahms' song. "The Blacksmith", unexpectedly, as in Haydn's "Surprise Symphony" or harmonically, as in the first four bars of Beethoven's "Sonata Pathètique". The children can also try to create their own climaxes on the drum either through pattern and speed, or through an increase or decrease of tone.

All this can lead us to listening to selected pieces from Schumann's "Albums for the Young", or Grieg's "Lyric Pieces Op. 12", for these selections illustrate a variety of musical moods which the children can express either by the way they move or by the pictures they draw. They can tell us whether they think the music sounds happy, sad, sleepy, lively, angry, or triumphant. Children are very quick to discover when music is loud (forte) or soft (piano) and in addition to learning these words, they will enjoy hearing the more interesting "fortissimo" for very loud, and "pianissimo" for very soft music. Again, they can be asked to illustrate loudness and softness in the way they move, conduct, sing, or play a percussion instrument. It is worth showing them a piece of music so that they can see how the person who is playing is shown by the words forte or piano, (or just *f* or *p*) when to play the music loudly, or softly. Fast and slow music is also easy for children to pick out, and at the same time they can learn four more attractive musical terms. *Presto* (quickly) and *Lento* (slowly); *Accelerando* (to quicken up and *Rallentando* (to slow down). Again, they can portray these terms by moving, playing instruments, or conducting. Movement is usually the most popular portrayal and trains, cars, ships or airplanes are usually the most popular choice.

When listening to loud and soft music, you can ask the children whether they hear an emphasis or louder tone on some of the notes and not others. They can clap on the louder beat and find out whether the music is saying *loud soft*[2], *loud soft soft*[3], *loud soft soft soft*[4], *or loud soft soft soft soft*[5]. They can learn that this emphasis is called an *accent* and looks like this $\diagdown$. I find that they like to listen to a short piece of music and instead of clapping or conducting the accents, draw them as they occur, in their books. I sometimes ask whether their mother uses "accent salt" in her cooking, and point out that accent salt intensifies the flavour of food, just as a musical accent intensifies the sound of music.

Having considered how speed and intensity add to the interest of music, children can listen to music played in a *staccato* and *legato* manner and be asked to show which type of music we are playing by the way they move. Did the jumpy music sound like walking with bare feet on hot sand? Was it like the way their pussy cat walks when she goes out in the snow for the first time? Was the smooth music like skating or sliding on a smooth floor? We can then get their books and as I play the staccato music they go ● ● ● in their books. They find this great fun and they can also draw the legato music as it is played with a series of curved lines, like phrase marks.

These two new words are written in their books and I make sure that in their next movement session, I introduce some legato and staccato music to see whether they recognize it and remember the names! Again it is worthwhile showing them a piece of music so that they can see that staccato notes have a dot over them and that the very smooth legato phrases are often marked with a curved line such as they have been drawing.

STACCATO

Hop hop hop and nev-er stop sta-cca-to sta- cca- to

LEGATO

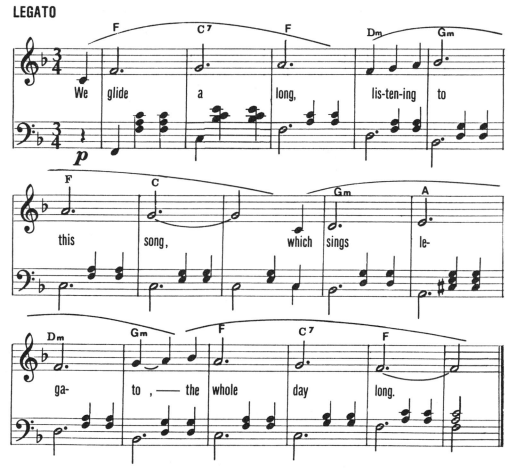

We glide a long, lis-ten-ing to

this song, which sings le-

ga- to, —— the whole day long.

Children also enjoy listening to *trills* and *glissandos* on the piano and then trying to play them and draw them:

[1] Cresendo for Percussion from Antigone, which can be found on the record, "The Love of Experience" Deutsche Gramaphone 2530.482.

Another "musical enrichment" can come when music changes from the major to the minor key. Get the children to listen to two verses of the song, "Go Tell Aunt Rhodie", and ask them to tell you when they notice something different. Play verse one in its original major key, but put verse two in a minor key. The children usually say that the tune now sounds "sadder". Play a variety of major and minor key changes, and see how many they can spot. You can tell them that major and minor music is based on the major or minor scales, and scales provide "patterns", like a knitting or crochet pattern, from which people make up melodies. You can play some scales if they are interested, and for your own benefit you can remember that it is the third of the scale that gives it its character (the "major" or larger third with four semitones and the "minor" or smaller third with only three semitones).

GO TELL AUNT RHODY (Major Key)

American Folk Song

gos- lings are cry- ing be- cause their moth-er's dead.

Having stressed the *enjoyment* value of these musically enriching aspects, I should also like to suggest that they are *important*, because through them the children can share in an emotional experience involving tension, relaxation, joy, and possibly grief, and such an experience helps the child to grow in emotional maturity.

Musical Form

It is inevitable that the shape or form of music is linked with the manner in which music is played, and it is also inevitable that form and shape concern children, whether they are consciously aware of it or not.

At its simplest, children are concerned with phrasing. When they sing one of their favourite nursery rhymes, they find that they have to pause somewhere to take a breath, and if they pause where the music naturally makes a pause because of the sense of the words, this makes taking a breath easy.

Just for fun we try singing a nursery rhyme without taking a breath, say our old favourite, "Lavender's Blue Dilly Dilly". We then find where we need to breathe and find that this fits in with the pattern of the melody: "Lavender's blue dilly dilly/Lavender's green" (breathe); "When I am King dilly dilly/You shall be Queen" (breathe). (It is also possible to breathe at the end of each line.) We sing other songs and find that the music suggests where to take a breath. Then we try walking to a song or a piece of music and pausing, or turning to walk in the opposite direction, when we hear the little break in the music denoting a breath or the end of a musical phrase. In addition to walking songs, the children like to take their books and draw a picture of the phrases as they occur, i.e.

From the shape of phrasing which is common to all music, we can move to the shape of the majority of folk and traditional songs: *A B* (binary) form, and *A B A* (ternary) form.

Taking a song like "Ah Si Mon Moine Voulait Dancer*", we can ask the children to listen to it and try to tell us why it is like a sandwich. To help them we can suggest that they clap when they hear the first tune, conduct when they hear the beginning of a new tune, and clap again if the first tune returns. They may then tell you, or you may point out, that tune one equals a piece of bread and butter, tune two, a filling, and the return of tune one, implies another piece of bread and butter. If we then play "Donkey Riding" they will discover that the first melody is *not* repeated. So this is an open-faced sandwich.

*In this book "Oh, come my top, will you dance with me."

DONKEY RIDING

Canadian Folk Song

Binary Form A. B.   The "Donkey" refers to the Donkey-engine not the animal

Were you ever in Cardiff Bay
Where the folk all shout Hurray!
Here comes John with his three months pay
Riding on a donkey

The children can listen to a number of tunes and say or draw the type of sandwich they think it is. When they draw the tune I write *A B* or *A B A* beside their drawing, saying that this is an easy and short way of saying what kind of tune (or sandwich) it is. I get some wonderful pictures, and the children often tell me at the next class that they have heard a musical sandwich on the radio! If the children have enjoyed this experience, and if the group is older and fairly musical, it is possible to embark on the double-decker sandwich! This consists of tune *A*, a new tune *B*, the return of *A*, followed by a new tune *C*. Tune *A* is again repeated and another new tune *D* follows, and so on; this is known as *Rondo* form, and in addition to individual pieces such as Beethoven's "Ecossaisse", many of the final movements of Beethoven's sonatas are in this form.

A child appreciates the shape of a tree without really knowing why it is so satisfying and, although a certain amount of information adds to her enjoyment, if we dissect the tree (in botanical terms) in *too* much detail, she gets bored and does not enjoy her tree anymore. the same applies to musical form. Do not go into too much detail. There is also a further similarity. If the shape of the tree is wrong, the child, although she would not know why, would be unhappy. Similarity, a musical composition which has no sense of form or musical shape would feel wrong, even if the child had no idea what was the matter.

A satisfying musical composition, however simple, needs: phrases that balance; some repetition, so that there is a sense of security; a climax, however simple; and a satisfactory ending. Again taking "Lavender's Blue Dilly Dilly" as our example, we find that it has four balancing phrases, the second phrase move one note higher than the first phrase, giving us a small climax; the third phrase repeats the first phrase giving this sense of security; and the final phrase finishes it off with the melody dropping to the home sound. It is all very simple and very satisfying.

Because *cadences* or chord endings help to define the shape of a song or a piece of music, we might let some of the older children listen to them and see if they can hear whey they do. The *perfect cadence*, (where the chord moves from the fifth degree of the scale to the first or eighth degree, the home sound) usually occurs at the end of a song, and it sounds final, as if the tune has really finished. The children hear this cadence in their "sit down" and "stand up" signals, and because of its finality it is fairly easy to recognize. The *imperfect cadence* (where the chords move from the first or eighth degree of the scale to the fifth) may occur in the middle of a song. The cadence sounds unfinished, as if the tune wants to continue.

(1) PERFECT	(2) IMPERFECT	(3) INTERRUPTED	(4) PLAGAL
V I	I V	V VI	IV I

The *interrupted cadence* (whose chords move from the fifth degree of the scale to the sixth or second degree, or to anything except the first or eighth degree), sounds interrupted, and this cadence usually occurs when one expects an ending and then the ending is not there! It is fun to play it sometimes when the children are expecting the perfect cadence for a sit down signal, just to see what they do! It is quite a logical cadence to play as it interrupts what they are doing, although it does not suggest what they do next. Another final cadence that the teacher might be aware of is the *plagal cadence* (whose chords move from the fourth degree to the first or eighth degree of the scale). As it sounds like an *Amen* it is sometimes called the Amen cadence, and can be used instead of the perfect cadence to make an ending.

Children are often more aware of stylistic differences in music than we realize, and a further listening experience can relate to different musical styles. Children can be asked to listen to two musical extracts, one popular and one classical, or two extracts, both of which can be classical, or both of which can be popular. A short pause is allowed between the two extracts, and the child is then asked whether item two is a continuation of item one — or is it something new? If it is new, is it similar in character to item one, or quite different? This is an excellent "listening test" for children aged seven to nine and those children who learn music through painting do exceptionally well (for further exploration of this, see the work of Prof. Klara Kern).

If and when songs that the children have been singing are accompanied by themselves on the melody instruments, the chime bars or the auto harp, it is usually by chords, so in addition to helping them to hear these "clumps" of notes they want to be able to sing a melody and hear another melody above (*a descant*) or below (an *alto* part) the melody they are singing. This is really the beginning of *contrapuntal* (one melody against another) music, and it is surprising how quickly the children are able to hold their melody, once they are aware of what is happening. This leads to the singing of easy rounds, and it is at this stage that their singing can be helped so much by singing as a family at home. It would be wonderful if all parents learned alto parts or descants (if they are unable to put them in spontaneously) so that when all the family are home or travelling in the car, they can sing, not in unison which becomes a little dull, but in parts.

I always sang around the house as I worked, and as soon as my children learned the tunes of the songs, I would sing a descant, or put in an alto part. As they all thought the other parts were more interesting than the melody, it was not long before they knew them too or tried putting in their own; with the result that one day when I started a song and gaily branched into the second part, each child changed too, and there was a yell of protest, "Mother, for heaven's sake, sing the tune!"

When making music with young children one does not expect to get involved in any of the more elaborate musical forms. However, for our own interest it is worth noting that the *minuet* and *trio* form, which constantly appears in Beethoven sonatas, or in symphonies when we go to concerts, is just a glorified musical sandwich, for the minuet is *A B A*, the trio is *A B A*, and if the minuet is repeated, which is usual, the whole forms one big *A B A*, or tenary composition.

It is sometimes interesting to plan music around the life of a composer, such as Beethoven, Schubert, Benjamin Britten, etc., and if we want to devote some time to one composer, the following program outline might be considered. A brief story of his life can be told, and the children can sing one or two of his songs; they can play one of his more simple melodies on a melodic instrument; listen to a piece of his music which tells a story or describes a mood, dramatizing or painting it, whichever they like; finally they can play one or two of his pieces scored for percussion band. To avoid too much sitting down these items can be interpersed with drumming and moving to a selection of the composer's more exciting rhythms.

Obviously, in this chapter I relate the child's first experience in expression, dynamics and form to the more classical approach to music. Many teachers, however, may choose to relate these experiences directly to today's young composers which probably means including some electronic compositions. Such an approach is certainly viable and may relate well to the children of today. There is really no choice between the so-called "classical" and "modern" music for both are music and the child will hear and meet both; the decision is simply one of when and how, and of our own preference.

DECK THE HALLS

Carol

Bars 1-2 Make a circle, move into
the centre raising arms.
Bars 3-4 Circle around.
Bars 5-8 Repeat actions g 1-4

Bars 9-10 Hang a bell round partner's neck.
Bars 11-12 Circle around.
Bars 13-14 Stand still.
Bars 15-16 Circle around and finally bow.

Music and the other Arts

Your child uses all the avenues of her senses simultaneously in order to understand and come to terms with the world in which she lives. She does not try to distinguish between singing, chanting, dancing, dramatizing, or drawing, as she moves from one medium to another in her attempt to express her feelings about, or her interest in, some particular thing; it is only the adult who makes an arbitrary distinction between the arts. Thus music and the arts "belong" and each can assist and enrich the other in the learning process. Even though in this chapter we consider the arts separately, by the end of the chapter I hope you will see how impossible it is to separate them. In fact, an equally suitable title for this chapter could be, "An Enriched Music Program".

Children who enjoy songs and singing also enjoy poetry, which needs to be read aloud or recited, just as songs need to be sung, and there are as many different types of poetry from which we can choose, as there are songs:

● Long narrative poems which tell a story;

● Poems which describe a certain mood;

● Poems which are lovely to listen to because of their choice of words;

● Poems that talk about something that especially interests children;

● Nonsense poetry and of course, the very short nursery rhyme or jingle.

Naturally you would not choose a long narrative poem unless it tells the kind of story that will interest children. Even then, having told them something about the story, it is probably better to select certain sections rather than read the whole poem. We would also, from a musical point of view, want to link such a poem with a piece of music.

For example, Longfellow's "Hiawatha" has a wonderful story and can provide a setting for the playing and singing of North American Indian music. Matthew Arnold's "Forsaken Merman" provides another long narrative poem with a fascinating story about mermaids and mermen. It contains some vivid descriptions of the sea and Mendelssohn's "Fingal's Cave" can supply just the right music to go with it. The poem talks about the waves in terms of "Now the wild white horses, play, champ, and chafe, and toss in the spray", and in the music you can hear the rise and fall of the waves as they gradually build up and rush into the cave. (If any children have never seen the sea, they can imagine a very large lake when a sudden wind ruffles its water and blows it into large and sometimes very dangerous waves).

There are many "mood" poems — for example, the one from "The Wind Has Wings", called "Orders", (see Appendix VIII, Bibliography).

> Muffle the wind
> Silence the clock
> Curb the small talk
> Cure the hinge squeak
> Banish the thunder
> Let me sit silent
> Let me wonder.
>
> — A.M. Klein

and there are many, many poems which depend on alliterations or their choice of words to express what they want. Here is a lovely one by Laura E. Richards, called, "The Baby Goes to Boston", and I have chosen it because it is not only an excellent example of alliteration, but it provides a "chorus" which everyone can chant.
(*Chorus*)

Loky, moky, poky, stoky, smoky, choky, chee.

What does the train say?
Jiggle, joggle, jaggle, joggle,
What does the train say?
Tiggle, joggle, jee.
Will the little baby go
Riding with the locomo — (*chorus*)

Ting, ting the bell rings
Ring for joy because we go
Riding with the locomo — (*chorus*)

Look how the trees run
Each chasing t'other one
Are they running for to go
Riding with the locomo? — (*chorus*)

Over the hills now
Down through the vale below
All the cows and horses run
Crying "Won't you take me on?" — (*chorus*)

So-So the miles go
Now it's fast and now it's slow
When we're at our journey's end
Say goodbye to snorting friend — (*chorus*)   *Laura E. Richards*

If you need music for this poetry I suggest you find a record or tape on train sounds, for example, "Departure" by Prokofiev.

Of course, children love nonsense poetry and in Canada we have some wonderful examples in Dennis Lee's "Alligator Pie". However, nonsense poetry goes back for longer than this — and I think we might look at Edward Lear's poems particularly, "Calico Pie" (see selection of jingles following this chapter) which is not only fun to say together but lends itself to body percussion or the playing of perscussion instruments.

Naturally, the younger the child, the shorter the poem and even babies from eighteen months on, enjoy short rhythmic rythmes or jingles.

I often start a music circle with a short poem or jingle which can relate to a number of different things. For example: the weather, the time of the year, what we are going to do now, what the child has already been doing.

The use of such poems or jingles is threefold: first, they provide an easy link with what the children have been doing before they come to music, secondly, they help the children to "settle down", and thirdly, if the children repeat them all together, or perhaps some of them will want to recite them on their own, they provide an opportunity for finding out who can memorize easily, who has a good sense of rhythm and timing and who finds difficulty with certain words or letters.

If you look through the "jingles" you will find some lovely theme verses for the fall and a variety of sound and idea jingles.

If the lesson theme is going to deal with "Quick and Slow Music", then "The Snail and the Mouse", or "The Steam Roller" provide us with excellent introductions. On the other hand, if we are going to have an animal theme, such as a pussy cat or a lion or tiger, then "Tiger Creeping through the Night" is fun to use, or the following poem:

> Walk, walk, softly slow,
> This is the way the tigers go,
> Walk, walk, get out of the way,
> Tigers are coming to school today!
> Creep, creep, softly slow,
> This is the way the tigers go,
> Creep, creep, come and play
> Tigers are coming to school today! *Scott*

Jingles, as well as longer poems, can be used to introduce music to which we want the children to listen, for example: "Winter" can introduce Debussy's "The Snow is Dancing". The two poets R.L. Stevenson and A.A. Milne may be dated in their descriptions of nurses and nurseries, however, both are great favourites and you can always find a poem which is relevant to today's child. Stevenson's "How Do You Like to Go Up in a Swing" is wonderful for movement, (swaying up and down, and then from side to side), while Milne's "John had Great Big Waterproof Boots on" lends itself to clapping and/or marching and it can be turned into a verse and chorus poem by dividing it up into four groups, for example:

(Group 1) John had/great big waterproof boots on (Group 2)
(Group 1) John had/a great big waterproof hat (Group 3)
(Group 1) John had/a great big waterproof macintosh (Group 4)
(Everyone) And that, said John, is that!

Lullabies as we already know, are very important, not only for babies, but for young children as well, and sometimes one can use a poem as a lullaby instead of singing or playing one. Here is a very lovely Indian lullaby.

O whispering breeze, sway her to sleep
with thy sleep-laden wings   )*bis*
This tiny bud drowsily sleeps, rocking, rocking to rest.
O whispering breeze sway her to sleep
with thy sleep-laden wings

O moonlight shine on this child of mine
Lull her, lull her to sleep.
O whispering breeze sway her to sleep)
with thy sleep laden wings.   )*bis*

Moving from poetry to *drama* — I think we would all agree that it is almost impossible to have a music class with young children *without* using drama in some form or another.

Songs such as "Jack and Jill" and "Sing a Song of Sixpence simply ask to be dramatized and we can all think of many of our favourite songs which the children love because they are able to "act them out"

In selecting music for dramatization, you can hardly do better than use pieces from Schumann's "Scenes from Childhood", or Kabalevsky's "Children's Pieces". You can also dramatize quite a long piece of music such as Grieg's "Spring" or "The Hall of the Mountain King", provided you are prepared to make up a convincing story about the music before they listen to it and dramatize it. It is also equally good, if not better, to get the children to listen to the music and make up their *own* stories to it, in which case one or two of their stories can be chosen for everyone to dramatize.

Dancing, which grows out of children's movement to music is, again, so much part of music that it needs very little explanation or encouragement.

The children dance when they sing some of their songs, such as, "Off We Go on our Ponies" or "It's Blowing" and they certainly dance when they participate in singing games. However, by the time they are 5 or 6 they also enjoy the type of dance which has a set pattern and some set steps, and if we cannot find the kind of dance we want in some book or other, we and our children should make up our own dances.

A very easy one, which I made up, can be danced to "I's the B'y" and there are several other Canadian folk songs which lend themselves to simple dance patterns, for example: "There's lots of fish in Bonavist' Harbour" or "If my top will dance with me". You can use tambourine dances for Spanish or Mexican programs, minuets for Haydn or Mozart programs and, of course, dances to carols — for the word "carol" means "to dance in a circle" — and all the old folk carols were meant to be danced, (In this chapter you will find examples of the dances I have mentioned here — and I hope they will inspire you to choreograph your own.)

I have never forgotten the children's reaction when I invited one of their mothers, who I knew was a dancer from New Delhi, India, to come and teach us an Indian dance. First of all, she told the children the story of the dance, then she showed them the meaning of the hand and body movements, then she suggested that they copy her and try to *do* the dance.

I was amazed at how quickly the children picked up her beautiful movements and gestures, which were quite intricate, and how much they enjoyed trying to remember the sequence of the various hand movements.

We didn't have music for this dance so she hummed the melody and accompanied herself with a small drum and it all worked out beautifully. Perhaps this is something to keep in mind, to find a parent or friend who dances professionally and invite them to take charge of a session with the children.

Here is a charming poem, by Eleanor Farjeon, to close our dance section:

Dancing
A hop, a skip and off we go
Happy ear and merry toe
Up and down and in and out
This way, that way, round about
Bend like grasses in the breeze
Wave your arms like wind-blown trees
Dart like swallows, glide like fish —
Dance like anything you wish!

I'SE THE B'Y

Newfoundland Folk Song
Choreography Barbara Cass Beggs

I'se the b'y that builds the boat and I'se the b'y sails her

I'se the b'y that catch-es the fish, and takes them home to Li- sa.

Chorus.

Hip yer part- ner Sal-ly Ti-bo' Hip yer part- ner Sal-ly Brown.

Fo- go, Twil-lin-gate Mor-tons har-bour all- a-round the cir- cle.

Form a circle and circle right—bars 1-4. Turn left and circle left bars 5-8. Move into the centre and clap bars 9-10. Move out and clap bars 11-12. Move into the circle again and clap bars 13-14 Then turn around as you go out of the centre, clap and bow.

TAMBOURINE DANCE

Music: Tambourine Dance La Traviata G. Verdi

Choreography Evy Paraskevopolous

(Children run in to tremolo on the piano)

Tambourines

A. Children move into the centre of the circle (run out again) twice, while beating tambourines.

B. Children shake tambourines high up with hand,   placing the other on their waist. Turn around while shaking and
bow on final chord.

C. Repeat actions to A and end with two forte beatings, children run out, shaking tambourines to tremolo on piano.

SCARF DANCE

Melody - Traditional
Choreography: Barbara Cass Beggs

A. wave wave wave wave

wave wave wave wave

B. sway sway turn around bow.

wave wave wave bow throw scarf

Each child holds a scarf and stands in a circle, or if preferred move round the room.
Bars 1-2 wave scarf in circular motion with right hand
Bars 3-4 turn round, while waving scarf.
Repeat the same movements for the next 4 bars.
Bars 9-12 Catch each end of scarf and hold over head while swaying from left to right.
Bars 13-16 Repeat first 4 bars and close with a bow or curtsey.
The scarves can then be thrown in the air and caught!

Now let's look at drawing, crayoning and *painting* types of art which at first may seem further removed from music than poetry or dancing. Yet this is not really the case, as those who have experimented in this field, such as Dr. Klara Kern from Vienna, have discovered.

In my *Listen, Like Learn* pre-school music program, we have made considerable use of art in various forms in our children's work books. When they listen to music which tells a story, or expresses a mood, we ask them to draw or paint that story or mood — sometimes they like to illustrate a song which they know and enjoy, and musical dynamics, which is discussed in another chapter, can certainly be illustrated in a variety of ways.

Colour shading — light for soft and a deeper or darker colour for loud, can indicate the progression of a crescendo – and to paint or crayon the music. "Crescendo" by Orff, having first listened to it and played along with it using rhythm sticks or drums, provides a new and exciting experience (see chapter 10).

Sometimes nonsense verses or poems are better understood if the child can illustrate them — painting music certainly provides another dimension to music and to me the value lies in the ability of the exercise to increase the child's listening capacity.

Finally, there is one other aspect of the arts which is worth considering and that is the need to cultivate the children's taste for pictures. Children like looking at pictures and when selecting books you can choose those with beautiful and interesting pictures which will appeal to children (and nowadays so many excellent artists illustrate our books). Children also learn to love pictures by looking at them on walls, by being given them to put up in their rooms and by being taken to picture galleries — as we take them to concerts. (Remembering that both for concerts and picture galleries, a "little at a time" is probably best.)

Sometimes we teach in a room which has no pictures or the pictures are poor artistically and can say little to the child. In this case, it is worthwhile pinning up some posters and certainly today there are some wonderfully attractive posters, which we can take down again when we have finished teaching.

When I taught in my own house I found the children noticed not only the pictures — but my books and ornaments — "what's this, and where does it come from?" they would ask, "why does that man have no clothes on?" (Michaelangelo's "David"). "Why do those children wear such funny clothes?" ("Children at Play" — Breughel).

I remember how much I enjoyed *my* music lessons as a child, not only because I enjoyed the actual lesson, but because my teacher's room contained many beautiful objects that she had collected on her travels — her pictures were modern, and to me exciting; and there was a sense of uncluttered beauty about the whole room which I found very restful. There is no question that children's behaviour is influenced by their surroundings; babies find a room in someone's home less alarming than a big hall: a drab, dirty or untidy room or hall has a very depressing effect; and badly treated books or instruments simply ask for more of the same kind of treatment!

When I taught at the Toronto University Settlement Music School, I found that the rooms allotted to our music school were not only somewhat dirty and messy, but the walls were painted yellowy-brown, the doors were brown and very scratched and marked, and there were no curtains. As I was not given any money to improve these rooms — I met with my staff and suggested that between us we get some paint and brushes and hold a weekend painting bee! Luckily, everyone was in agreement and by the time the children came, each room was painted a different pastel colour, the doors were white, and there were some colourful pictures up. A final touch, made possible by one of the staff who had a sewing machine, was cheap, but attractive curtains on the windows. I was told by the resident staff that it was probably a waste of time — that children would soon damage the rooms — we thought otherwise! And we were right! For the children loved the rooms, took great care of everything and I'm sure were able to understand and enjoy their music better because of the atmosphere of the rooms. Young children are particularly sensitive to moods and atmosphere — and given a messy, untidy room, they will be messy and untidy! This unified approach to music teaching has not yet been adopted in general. However, it is so successful that in time I am sure more music teachers will consider it. To quote again from "Learning Through Movement" (see book list), "Music, visual art and movement are closely related art forms . . . each shares the opportunity to assist children in developing self-awareness, creative expression, and the capacity to esthetically experience their own beings and their environment".

SUGGESTED MUSIC

SAD from *Death and Maiden* by Schubert
SURPRISED from *The Surprise Symphony* by Haydn
CRESCENDO and DIMINUENDO from *Symphony No. 1* by Brahms
STACCATO from *The Clock Symphony* by Haydn
CHORDS: any Bach chorale
MELODY from *The Sonata for Violin and Piano* (Spring Sonata) by Beethoven
TRIUMPHANT from *See the Conqu'ring Hero Comes* by Handel
RESTFUL from *Nocturn* from *Midsummer Night's Dream* by Mendelssohn
A CANON from *Symphony No. 4* by Beethoven
A SONG from *Symphony No. 9* (Choral) *Ode to Joy* by Beethoven
All of the above extracts can be found in *Famous Tunes Arranged for Piano*
(Books Ia, Ib, 11a, 11b) by John Wilson, Oxford University Press.

ANGRY from *Anger over a Lost Penny* by Beethoven
HAPPY from *Rondo in F* by Beethoven
LIVELY from *Turkish March* by Beethoven
CHARMING from *Minuet and Trio in G* by Beethoven
These four extracts can be found in *Beethoven* by Opal Wheeler, E.P. Dutton
Co. Inc.

FAIRIES from *Fairies Dance* by Grieg
WATCHMEN (a castle, a storm, or giants) from *The Watchman* by Grieg
These two extracts can be found in "Lyric Pieces Op. 12", Grieg

LEGATO from *Melody* by Schumann
A GLIDER from *Humming Song* by Schumann
MAJESTIC or GIANTS from *Northern Song* by Schumann
A JET PLANE from *Knight Rupert* by Schumann
HORSES GALLOPING from *The Wild Horses* by Schumann
These five extracts can be found in *Album for the Young* Op. 68, Schumann

CLOWNS or FUNNY from *Clowns* by Kabalevsky
MOVING QUICKLY from *Running Along* by Kabalevsky
SLEEPING from *Cradle Song* by Kabalevsky
TWINS and BIG BROTHERS from *The Little Twins* by Kabalevsky
CHEERFUL or A HELICOPTER from *A Gay Little Story* by Kabalevsky
These five extracts can be found in *Twenty-four Little Pieces for the Piano* by
Dimitri Kabalevsky. If an example of a fugue or nine or twelve-eight time are
required these can be found in Book I of *Forty-Eight Preludes
and Fugues* by J.S. Bach.

SUGGESTED MUSIC FOR LISTENING

Bach: *Air on a G String*
Jesu, Joy of Man's Desiring

Beethoven: *Choral Symphony No. 9 (third movement)*
Minuet in G
Moonlight Sonata (first movement)
Fifth Symphony (first movement)
Spring Sonata No. 5 Op. 25 (first movement)
Pastoral Symphony No. 6 (slow movement)
Ecossaises

Bizet: *Suite No. 1 Carmen*
Brahms: *Hungarian Dances*
Britten: *The Storm*
Borodin: *The Dances from Prince Igor*
Clarke: *Trumpet Voluntary*
Copeland: *Rodeo*
Debussy: *The Children's Corner* and *La Mer*
Dukas: *The Sorcerer's Apprentice*
Dvorak: *New World Symphony (movement in 5 time)*
Slavonic Dance No. 8
Elgar: *Nursery Suite*
Grainger: *Shepherd's Hey*
Grieg: *Peer Gynt Suite*
Grovlez: *L'Almanach aux Images* (Donkey and Doll's Lullaby)
Haydn: *The Toy Symphony*
Herbert: *March of the Toys*
Holst: *Saint Paul's Suite* and *The Planets*
Humperdinck: *Hansel and Gretel Music*
Kodály: *Harry Janos Suite*
Mozart: *Concerto for Horn No. 3 (third movement)*
Sonata in A Major (theme)
Symphony in G Minor (opening theme)
Eine Kleine Nachtmusik
Mendelssohn: *Incidental Music, Midsummer Night's Dream (scherzo)*
Overture to the Hebrides (Fingal's Cave)
Prokofiev: *Peter and the Wolf*
Purcell: *Golden Sonata*
Paganini: *Moto Perpetuo*
Poldinine: *Dancing Doll*
Quilter: *The Children's Overture*
Ravel: *Mother Goose Suite*
Respighi: *The fountains of Rome*
Rimsky-Korsakov: *The Flight of the Bumble Bee*
Strauss: *Thunder and Lightning Polka*
Saint-Saens: *The Carnival of the Animals (The Elephant, The Lions, The Swans)*

Schubert: *Unfinished Symphony (first movement)*
Ballet Music – Dance from Rosamunde
Military March
Variations from the Trout Quintet
Schumann: *Album for the Young*
Sibelius: *Finlandia*
Tchaikovsky: *1812 Overture*
The Nutcracker Suite
Villa-Lobos: *The Little Train of the Brazilian Countryside*
Vivaldi: *The Four Seasons*

Many of these suggestions and some additional ones can be found in Adventures in Music R.C.A. Victor, Vol. 1 and 2.

PERCUSSION POEMS

drum	One is a giant who stamps his feet
triangle	Two is a fairy, light and neat
bell	Three is a mouse who is oh so small
tambourine	Four is a great big bouncing ball.

CALICO PIE

Instrument	Sing	Body Percussion
Bells	Calico pie The little birds fly Down to the calico tree, Their wings were blue And they sang "tilly-loo"? Till away they flew —	*Snap fingers*
Rhythm Sticks	And they never came back! They never came back! They never came back to me!	*Clap*
Tambourine	Calico jam The little fish swam Over the syllabub sea, He took off his hat To the sole and the sprat, And the willeby-wat — But he never came back to me!	*Hit knees*
Rhythm Sticks	He never came back! He never came back! He never came back to me!	*Clap*

Triangles	Calico ban.	*Wave hands*
	The little mice ran.	*to sh-sh*
	To be ready in time for tea,	
	Flippity flup,	
	They drank it all up	
	And danced in the cup —	
	But they never came back to me!	
Rhythm	They never came back!	*Clap*
Sticks	They never came back!	
	They never came back to me!	
Drum	Calico drum,	*Stamp feet*
	The grasshoppers come	
	The butterfly, beetle, and bee.	
	Over the ground	
	Around and around,	
	With a hop and a bound, —	
	But they never came back to me!	
Rhythm	They never came back!	*Clap*
Sticks	They never came back!	
	They never came back to me!	
		Edward Lear

FEET

Drum	*Big feet, black feet, going up and down the street*	Stamp
	Dull and shiny Father's feet, walk by me.	
Tambourine	Nice feet, brown feet, going up and down the street	*Walk*
	Pretty, dainty Mother's feet, trip by me	
Bells	Small feet, light feet, going up and down the street	*Run*
	Little children's happy feet, run by me.	

	Two little sausages frying in a pan	
tone block/	One went pop and the other went bang.	*Drum*

	A box of rice krispies	*Rub Hands*
	Sitting in a shop	
	Some went crackle and some went pop.	*Snap fingers*

Tambourine	Two little lion cubs sitting on the floor	
	One went wuff	
	and the other went roar!	*Big drum*

SEASONS

Spring
The Spring is sprung
The grass is green —
The birds sing out
But are not seen.
The dandelions grow apace —
Each with a sunny, smiling face.

Summer
Summer breeze so softly blowing
In my garden plants are growing
If we have both sun and showers
Then my plants will turn to flowers.

The Fall
Apples round and apples red
Growing higher than my head
I'm picking apples from the tree
One for you and one for me.

Here is a tree with its leaves so green
Here are the apples that hang in between
When the wind blows the apples will fall
Here is a basket to gather them all.

Leaves are floating softly down
They make a carpet on the ground
When swish the wind comes whirling by
And sends them dancing to the sky.

Winter
Walk fast in snow, in frost go slow
And still as you go, tread on your toe.
When frost and snow are both together
Sit by the fire and spare shoe leather.

FINGER POEMS

A fat pig (thumb)
A short pig
A long pig
A thin pig
And a pig with a curly tail.

* * *

Fingers like to wiggle waggle, wiggle waggle, wiggle waggle way up high
Fingers like to wiggle waggle, wiggle waggle, wiggle waggle way down low
Fingers like to wiggle waggle, wiggle waggle, wiggle waggle on my knee

* * *

I have ten little fingers and they all belong to me
And I can make them do things, would you like to see?
I can shut them up tight, I can open them wide,
I can put them behind me and make them all hide.
I can make them jump high, I can make them jump low,
I can put them together, and fold them just so.

* * *

Said this little doggie I want to play (thumb)
Said this little doggie let's run today
Said this little doggie let's bark and bark
Said this little doggie let's stay out 'til dark
Said this little doggie I think t'would be fun (baby finger)
To take outselves home, so let's run, run, run.

* * *

Open shut and give a little clap,
Open shut and put them in your lap.

* * *

Creep up to the shoulders high
Like birds they flutter in the sky
Like leaves they fall down to the ground
Now pick them up and roll them round.

* * *

IDEA POEMS

What do you suppose
A bee sat on my nose
Then what do you think?
He gave a wink and said,
"I beg your pardon
I thought you were a garden."

* * *

Slice, slice, the bread looks nice
Spread, spread, the butter on the bread
On the top put jam so sweet
Now — it's nice to eat.

* * *

I like sugar, I like tea, I like you and you like me
I like Daddy, who's as tall as can be —
And I like sitting on my mummy's knee.

NUMBER POEMS

Here is bee hive, where are the bees?
Hiding away where nobody sees
They are coming out now,
They are all alive,
1, 2, 3, 4, 5!
(make a fist with your hand, then jump fingers up one at a time)

* * *

One, two, kittens that mew,
Two three, birds in a tree,
Three, four, shells on the shore,
Four, five, bees in a hive,
Five, six, a cow that licks,
Six, seven, birds in the heaven,
Seven, eight, sheep at the gate,
Eight, nine, clothes on the line,
Nine, ten, a little black hen.

* * *

Five little pussy cats
All black & white
Sleeping so peacefully
All through the night
Lets wake them up —
Mew, mew, mew, mew, mew.
(Make a fist with your hand, then jump the fingers up one at a time)

ACTION POEMS

Here is a steam roller, rolling and rolling,
Ever so slowly because of its load
Then it rolls up to the top of the hill,
Puffing and panting it stands very still
Then it rolls all the way down!

* * *

An elephant goes like this, and that,
He's terribly big and he's terribly fat!
He has no fingers, he has no toes,
But goodness gracious!
What a nose!

* * *

Birds fly high, in the sky
To and fro, watch them go
Birds fly everywhere.

* * *

Slowly, slowly, very slowly creeps the garden snail
Slowly, slowly, very slowly, up the garden rail.
Quickly, quickly, very quickly creeps the little mouse
Quickly, quickly, very quickly round about the house.

* * *

Ten galloping horses, (both hands gallop up above your head)
Galloping through the town
Five galloped up (right hand gallops up)
And five galloped down (left hand gallops down)
Five were white (right hand gallops), and five were brown (left hand gallops).
Ten galloping horses galloping through the town (both hands gallop above your head).

* * *

Mix a pancake
Stir a pancake
Pop it in the pan
Fry the pancake
Toss the pancake
Catch it if you can

* * *

I wiggle my fingers
I wiggle my toes
I wiggle my shoulders
I wiggle my nose
Now no more wiggles are left in me
And I am as still as still can be

* * *

Topsy toe (touch toes)
Peggy leg (touch legs)
Nancy knee (touch knee)
And little me (touch body)

* * *

Fly little handies fly away high
Wave little handies wave to the sky
Dance little handies dance on my knee
Hide little handies – hide away from me.

* * *

Tiger creeping through the night
Tigers' eyes are very bright
Tigers' creeping very slow
When he sees you he says Wow!

Summary of the "Listen-Like-Learn" approach

The "Listen-Like-Learn" approach applies to children aged two to six, and is a three-year music course for beginners. "Listen-Like-Learn" may be started at any age, for if a child starts music classes at five or six or even eight or nine, she still needs to cover the basic preliminaries of the course. (She would naturally move more quickly if she started at 6 or 7, and the vocabulary used in the classes would be suitable to her age group). In general, it is important for all children to have a *group* experience of music where they are free to sing, move, improvise and discover what music is about, before starting to learn an individual instrument.

The actual content of the classes cover rhythm, melody, musical dynamics, form and expression. These are interpreted through singing (folk songs, and particularily Canadian folk songs), movement, creative dance, drama, poetry and painting or drawing. Emphasis is placed on "listening", which involves concentration. Musical notation related to the *Curwen* time names and solfége is introduced as soon as possible, and leads to basic sight-reading and the realization that music is a written as well as a listened-to-language.

Children learn to love and understand music through the richness and variety of music itself. This means that if the teacher responsible for music classes does not play an instrument, good recordings and tapes must be available.

Although musical ability is encouraged, the aim of these classes, particularily when presented as part of a pre-school programme, in play schools, daycare centres, or junior schools, is to assist the development of the whole child, so that through enjoying music she can gain a sense of self-confidence and security.

Any number of correct learning situations may be set up, but without a sense of shared enthusiasm and enjoyment, your child will accomplish little that is worthwhile.

Perhaps the most important thing about music-making with the young child is the ability to enjoy both making and listening to it, and this ability to enjoy needs to be "caught". Children catch the enjoyment of *listening* to music from an enthusiastic teacher in "Listen-Like-Learn" classes; they *like* music because it is play, it is fun; they *learn* music through the structured content of the classes.

Musical Terms

Musical terms are useful to know and some of them are fun for the children to learn if they are acquired as the children come to use them: e.g. when they move to *legato* or *staccato* or play the drum *forte* or *piano*. The reason why these terms are in Italian is because historically the Italians were first to make their mark in the musical field. The influence of their church and contrapunctual music was felt in England as early as the seventh century, and in Europe in general, by the ninth century. When later they composed *Oratorios* and *Operas*, moving from *contrapunctual* to *harmonic* style music, their influence became very widespread, and as musical terms became well established they were accepted as authoritative. In fact, one might say that musically, Italian became an international language.

Accelerando .... Gradually faster
Ad Lib .... At pleasure
Adagio .... Slow
Adagissimo .... Very slow
Affretando .... Hurrying
Agitato .... Agitatedly
Allargando .... Getting slower and stronger in tone
Allergo .... Lively, fast
Andante .... At a walking pace
Animato .... Animatedly
A piacere .... At pleasure
Appassionato .... Passionately
Assai .... Very
A tempo .... In time i.e. resuming normal speed after a deviation
Bene .... Well
Bis .... Twice
Breve .... Now, the longest note equal to four half notes (minims)
Brillante .... Brillant
Callando ..... Decreasing both in tone and speed
Cantabile .... In a singing style
Capo .... (lit, head), the beginning
Coda .... (lit, tail) A passage at the end of a movement, to make a good ending.
Come .... As
Con .... With
Crescendo ...... Gradually louder
Crotchet .... (Quarter note)
Da Capo or D.C. ... From the beginning
Dal Segno or D.S. .... From the sign
Decrescendo ... ... Gradually softer
Demisemiquaver (Thirty-second note)
Diminuendo .... Gradually softer
Dolce .... Sweetly
Dolente .... Sadly

Doppio momento .... Twice as fast
Energico .... With energy
Espressione .... Expression
Espressivo .... With expression
Facile .... Easy
Fine .... The end
Forte .... Loud
Fortissimo .... Very loud
Forzando .... Forcing
Furioso .... Furiously
Giocoso .... Gay
Glissando .... The rapid playing of of a scale passage by drawing the thumb or finger across the keys.
Grave .... Very slow and solemn
Grazioso .... Gracefully
Lamentoso .... Mournfully
Largo .... Slow
Legato .... Smooth
Leggiero .... Lightly
Lento .... Slow
L'istesso .... speed of the beat remains the same but the notation changes.
Lunga pausa .... Long pause
Ma .... But
Maestroso .... Majestically
Marcato .... marked
Meno .... Less
Meno mosso .... Less movement
Mezza voce .... At half voice
Mezzo .... Moderately
Mezzo-forte .... Moderately loud
Minim .... (half note)
Moderato .... Moderate time
Moto .... Movement
Non Tanto .... Not too much
Obbligato .... Indispensable
Opus .... A work, a published composition

Ossia .... Or
Ostinato .... A repeated tune
Parlando .... To be sung in a
    speaking manner
Pausa .... A rest
Ped ..... Depress the right sustaining
    pedal (*means release pedal)
Perendosi .... Dying away
Piano .... Soft
Pianissimo .... Very softly
    (-issimo added to an Italian word
    means very)
Piu .... More
Pizzicato .... Plucked
Poco .... A little
Portamento .... Gliding
Presto .... Very quickly
Primo .... First
Quaver .... ♪ (Eighth note)
Rallentando .... Becoming
    gradually slower
Replica .... Repetition
Risoluto .... Resolutely
Ritardando .... Gradually slower
Ritenuto .... Held back
Rubato .... "Stolen"
Temp Rubato, a portion of the duration
    taken from some notes and
    added to others the detail varies
    but the phrase length is normal.
Scherzando .... Playfully
Scherzo .... A joke
Semi-breve .... o (whole note)
Semi-quaver ...... ♪ (sixteenth note)
Semiplice .... Simply
Sempre .... Always
Sforzando .... Forcing
Simile .... In a like manner
Smorzando .... Forcing
Sosienuto .... Sustained
Sotto .... Below
Sotto voce .... In an undertone
Suave .... Smooth
Subito .... Suddenly

Tanto .... So much
Tempo .... The speed
Tenuto .... Held
Tranquillo .... Calmly, tranquilly
Tremolo .... A rapid repetition
    of a note or notes, a trill
Troppo .... Too much
Tutti .... All
Un, Una, Uno .... One
Una Corda .... One string
    (In piano music it indicates the left
    soft pedal)
Vibrato .... Vibrating
Vivace .... Lively

These terms are a basic selection and there are, of course many additional French and German terms. Any good book on the rudiments of music will supply additional term. (See Bibliography and resource list).

First lines of poems and jingles

Index to First Lines of Songs

Suggestions on Use of Poems to teach music to children

To introduce a new concept:
Loud-soft, Quick-slow, High-low

To help speech patterns:
Listen while the poem is read, imitate, say poem alone or in a group.

To improve rhythmic patterning:
Clap or play on rhythm sticks, discover loud and soft beats, clap pulse and patterns.

To encourage creative dramatization:
Let the children choose a poem or poems, dramatize in a group or individually. This could also include experiments with sound effects.

To enjoy as poems:
Use at the opening of a class or when moving from one subject to another, which leads to reading other poems, discussing poems, and asking the children to find a poem they like.

Instruments and ages

In the "Listen Like Learn" music classes the children meet, try to play, and with their parents' co-operation, are encouraged to choose what instrument they would like to play. Because these music classes provide an opportunity for discovering what music is about, when they come to learn the instrument of their choice, they can concentrate on the technique of that instrument, instead of having to meet everything — technique, rhythm, melody, notation, expression etc. all at the same time. This is why, if at all possible, music classes as such, should be considered as a pre-requisite for learning an instrument. Two to six years of age is the best for this type of musical participation and six and a half and seven years of age a good time for individual instrumental lessons. (Although I am glad to say that most teachers now include some group work as part of their individual lessons).

Many children are, of course, exceptions to age guidelines as they differ widely in desire and ability; however, here are some helpful suggestions regarding age and the selection of an instrument, although it is impossible to lay down a hard and fast rule in this respect.

Twos and threes

All the simple percussion instruments, chime bars, glockenspiels, xylophones, dulcimers (miniature glockenspiels) Montessori mushroom bells, the piano, auto harp and, in a Suzuki class, a violin. (At this age mothers or some assistants are needed to play along with the child, for it is no fun playing any instruments by ones' self!)

Fours and fives

At this age the children can find actual melodies on the piano and try to accompany their own singing on the autoharp. If their fingers are strong and well co-ordinated they can start serious piano lessons (at five) (with many lessons and a minimum of practice!) The treble or descant recorder can be started, and if they enjoy strumming on the autoharp, a ukulele (a small guitar-like instrument with four strings) and the chordal dulcimer, (where the strings are grouped so that they form chords) can be tried. They will continue to enjoy the instruments listed in the two to three age group the kazoo, (a toy instrument that the child blows and sings into) is fun.

Sixes and sevens

Continue with any of the instruments previously listed, and add the Orff xylophones and metalphones, which can continue to be used in work with the eights, nines and tens. The recorder and piano can now be treated seriously and some practice is necessary. As it is possible to obtain small violins and cellos this is an excellent time to start the string instruments, unless the child is already part of a Suzuki string group, in which case she will continue with this. The Spanish guitar is a possibility, particularly if they have "chord helper" on the guitar.

Eights, nines and tens

An alto recorder can be added, and if they are available the clavichord and harpsichord can be played, also the small Hammond organ. Some people who own a small organ start the children on this instead of the piano, (however it must be remembered that the technique of the organ is very different from that of the piano and it is difficult for a child to switch from one to the other.) If the child is interested in "blowing" instruments a flute, piccolo (a tiny flute) a B flat clarinet, or a cornet, (which in time can lead on to a trumpet. French horn or other Brass instruments) can be enjoyed. The harmonica or mouth-organ appeals about this time. Children can try playing this at the seven-eight age but it is more difficult than it appears. Like the recorder it is wonderful to play an instrument that is so easy to carry around! The harp or lyre (a small harp) can be enjoyed although these are expensive instruments and the harp is a difficult instrument to carry about! A variety of drums, particularly the type used in a dance band, steel band drums, military drums or some of the more complicated African drums also appeal at this age and to the six and seven year olds. Tubular bells (eight metal tubes strung from an upright frame) and the marimba (a sophisticated version of the xylophone) offer further opportunities.

Naturally, when selecting an instrument the physical characteristics of the child should be studied. A good ear (the ability to hear when music is at the correct pitch) is essential for string, woodwind and brass players who have to create their own musical sounds. A well-developed jaw and good breath control helps a woodwind or brass player. Finger stretch and strength are important for the cellist and harpist, and well-shaped fingers, a good stretch and muscular control certainly help pianists.

Learning an instrument of any kind is well worth while, even if the child will never qualify as a solo player and has not the musical ability to become a professional musician. Playing an instrument involves a co-ordination of mind and muscles , and the aural, tactile and visual faculties, while the effect of this training in co-ordination extends well beyond instrumental performance. Playing an instrument also provides a new skill and enjoyment and enriches the child's social and emotional life.

In this appendix on instruments and ages I have only mentioned the instruments which an average North American child would be likely to learn. A very different list of instruments would be presented if one looked at other parts of the world.

In Russia or the Ukraine a child might well study balalaika (a folk instrument with three strings). In India the tabla (a pair of drums) or one of the melody instruments the sitar, flute or sarangi. (the drone instrument is the tambura). In Japan or China the bamboo flute (or *shakuhachi*) or the *koto*, (a plucked string instrument). The Chinese instruments are similar but have different names. In Islamic music lyres, harps and zithers form an important part of the musical scene.

It is not my intention to suggest if and when these instruments can be studied. It is my intention to suggest that we can increase our enjoyment of music if we take any opportunity we can to listen to the music of instruments which are new and different from the ones to which we are accustomed.

Musical Pioneers

Zoltan Kodály: born in Hungary in 1882, a composer who also collected folk songs, and through their use revolutionalized musical education in Hungary. He devised a system based on these songs, and taught children to both sing and play their own folk music. He stressed the importance of sight reading and the voice and he was concerned with the whole personality of the child, stating that his goal in music teaching was to make children better musicians, which *per se* made them better human beings. He conducted experiments in the Hungarian schools which showed that children attending the schools which gave special attention and time to music, attained a higher academic record, not only in music, but in all their normal subjects. This was attributed to the fact that through music the children learned to concentrate and, as they enjoyed the music classes, they became more relaxed and more receptive to other subjects.

Carl Orff: born in Germany in 1895, a composer with a special interest in music with a strong rhythmic character which he carried over into his percussive approach to music teaching. He succeeded in changing people's attitudes to percussion instruments by making his own beautiful-sounding ones and he added much to children's enjoyment of ensemble playing and improvisation. He was less interested in sight-reading and the use of the child's voice.

Emile Jacques Dalcroze: a Swiss, born in Vienna in 1865, who worked out a system of training children through music and movement. He called his system Eurythmics" (*Eu* from the Greek meaning "good" or a sense of well-being). Although his concern was entirely with music, he has had considerable influence on modern and creative dance.

John Curwen: born in England in 1816. He founded the Tonic Sol-Fa system based on the early work of Guido d'Arezzo. This sytem, used by Kodály and many others, has improved sight-reading to a marked degree. He also introduced the time names of the Galin Parin Chévre method which helps children to hear and understand the time length of musical sounds.

Shinichi Suzuki: born in Japan in 1889, has developed a method of teaching the violin and other instruments to very young children. His method emphasizes listening, imitating, repeating and memorizing. Mothers must accompany their young children and learn along with them so that they can help them.

In addition to these pioneer musical teachers, we need to remember that psychologists and experts in the field of child education have also pioneered methods of teaching and demonstrated what a child is capable of learning at a given age. Language experts, too, have added their contribution for they have found that before he can write he needs to hear and experience a language. This confirms the experience of musicians who have found that before a child can read or play music, he needs to experience music through hearing it and expressing it in song and movement.

BIBLIOGRAPHY: Songs

A Musical Calendar of Festivals: Cass-Beggs, Barbara, Ward Lock Educational, London, England 1982.
A Treasury of Christmas Songs & Carols: Simon, Henry W. Houghton Mifflin Co., Boston, Mass. 1955.
Canadian Folk Songs for the Young: Cass-Beggs, Barbara, Douglas & MacIntyre, Vancouver, B.C. 1976.
Claredon Folk Song Books, 1 & 2: Clarendon Song Book Service, Oxford University Press, Toronto 1957.
Favourite French Folk Songs: Mills, Alan, Oak Publications, Embassy Music Corp., New York 1962.
Fifty Nursery Songs: Kodaly Zoltan, Boosey and Hawkes Inc., (English Edition) Torontó 1974.
Folk Carols for Young Children: Cass-Beggs, Barbara, Ward Lock Educational, London, England 1980.
Folk Lullabies for Young Children: Cass-Beggs, Barbara and Cass-Beggs, Michael, Oak Publications, Embassy Music Corp. New York 1969.
Folk Songs for Young Folk: Mills, Alan, Canadian Music Sales, Toronto 1957.
Folk Songs of Europe: Maud Karpeles, Novello & Co., 1956.
Jim along Josie: Nancy & John Langstaff, Harcourt Brace Jovanovick Inc. New York, 1970.
Harlequin: Gadsbury, David, A.C. Black, London, England 1981.
Lucille Panabaker's Song Book: Panabaker, Lucille. (Book 1 & 2) 1968.
New High Road of Song: Fletcher and Denison, W.J. Gage Co., Toronto 1972.
Nursery Songs of Other Lands: Anderson, Marion, Boosey and Hawkes Inc., Toronto 1946.
Oxford Nursery Song Book: Buck, Percy. Oxford University Press, Toronto 1933.
Sally Go Round the Sun: Fowke, Edith McClelland and Stewart, Toronto 1969.
Sing a Song One, Sing a Song Two: Bird, Wendy and McAuliffe, Gary: Nelson Ltd. London, England 1976.
Sixty Songs for Little Children and a Second & Third Sixty Songs: Clarendon Song Book Service, Oxford Univ., Press 1957.
Songs for the Nursery School: MacCarteney, Laura; Pendleton Willis Music Co., Cincinnati, Ohio., U.S.A. 1937.
Songs to Share: Haines Joan, G.V. Thompson Ltd., Toronto, Ontario 1964.
The Claredon Singing Games Books 1 & 2: Oxford Univ., Press, Toronto, 1957.
This Little Puffin: Matterson, Elizabeth, Penguin, 1969.

BIBLIOGRAPHY: Rhythmic Movement

Children Dancing: Shreeves, R; Ward Lock Educational, 1979.
Creative Movement for the developing Child: Cherry, Claire, Fearon Pub. California U.S.A. 1971.
Learning Through Movement: Werner, P.H. Burton, S.C., C.V. Musby Co., St. Louis, U.S.A., 1949.
Music and Movement: Driver, Ann; Oxford University Press, 1936.
Tunes With a Purpose: Anderson, Marion. Oxford Univ. Press, 1958.

BIBLIOGRAPHY: Percussion Instruments

(instruction books on how to make such instruments)

Making Musical Instruments: Mills and Boon, Lively Craft Cards, Pub. Peter Williams, Tonbridge Kent, U.K. 1971.
Musical Instruments from Odds and Ends, John Burton: Carousel Books, Trans World Pub. Ltd. London, U.K. 1976.
Musical Instrument Recipe Book, McGraw Hill Book Co., New York, 1971.

BIBLIOGRAPHY: SPECIAL SUBJECTS (Music & Song)

Carolare, The Little Fir Tree and Three Trains: Anderson, Marion, Oxford Univ. Press, Toronto (1946, 1954 & 1957).

BIBLIOGRAPHY: Misc. Music Courses

Creative Music for the Developing Child: Cherry Claire, Fearon Pub. Inc., Belmont, California, 1971.
La Musique et les Tout-Petits: Bromham, J. Katie, Gibaumont, Brussels, Belgium, 1963.
Leading Young Children to Music: Haines, J.; Gerber, L.; Columbus Merrill Pub. Co., N.Y. 1980.
Move, Sing, Listen, Play: Wood, Donna; Gordon, V.; Thompson Ltd. Toronto, Ontario, 1982.
Music as a Way of Life for the Young Child: Bayless and Ramsey Co., Toronto, Ontario, 1982.
Music and Perceptual Motor Development: Crewe, K.; Centre for Applied Research in Education, N.Y. 1975.
Music and Young Children: Arnoff, Frances Webber. Turning Wheel Press, New York, 1979.
Music Experiences in Early Childhood: Andres, Barbara. Holt Rhinehart & Winston, Toronto, Ontario, 1980.
Music for Children: Orff, Carl, Sennott & Co., N.Y. 1960.
Music for Fun, Music for Learning: Birkenshaw Lois Holt Rhinehard and Winston Canada Ltd., 1977.
Music for Young Children: Nye, Vernice. W.M.E. Brown & Co., Iowa U.S.A. 1975.
Musical Starting Points with Young Children: Gilbert, Jean. Ward Lock Educational. London, England, 1981.
Nurtured By Love, Shinichi Suzuki. Exposition Press, N.Y., U.S.A. 1969.
Orff-Schulwerk, Music for Children: Hall, Doreen. Schott & Co. London, England, 1960.
Rhythmic Music & Education: Dalcroze, Jacques. Putnam, N.Y. 1922.
Sound Beginnings: Churchley & Slind, McGraw-Hill, Toronto, Ontario, 1967.
The Kodály Method: Choksy, L.; Prentice Hall, New Jersey, U.S.A. 1974.
The Musical Experience of the Pre-School Child: Moog, Helmut. Schott & Co.,
London, England, 1976.

The New Curwen Method, Book 1: The Curwen Institute, London, England, 1980.

The Oxford School Music Books: Infant Book. Oxford University Press; London England, 1959.

What To Do Until the Teacher Comes: Glatt, Louise. Berandol Music Ltd. Toronto, Ontario, 1978.

Your Baby Needs Music: Cass-Beggs, Barbara. Douglas & MacIntyre, Vancouver, B.C. 1978.

BIBLIOGRAPHY: Child Development

Babyhood: Leach P.; Penguin Books, Middlesex, England, 1964.

The Activity of Children: Pickard, P.M. Longmans, London, England, 1965.

The Adult and the Nursery School Child: Fletcher, Margaret. University of Toronto Press, Toronto, 1969.

The Child and Reality: Piaget, Jean. Frederick Muller, London, England, 1971.

The Competent Infant: Stone L.J.; Comp. Tavistock Pub. Ltd. London, England, 1974.

The Child from Five to Ten Gessel, Arnold and Ilg, Frances. Harper and Row, New York, 1946.

The Growth of Musical Concepts in Young Children: Jones, M.L.; Glynn. Nat. Froebel. Foundation Bulletin 42, 1963.

The Magic Years: Fraiberg, Selma H.; Scribner's, New York 1959.

The Mental Growth of the Preschool Child: Gesell, Arnold and Ilg, Frances; Macmillan, New York, 1945.

The Nursery Years and the Psychological Aspects of Child Development: Isaacs, Susan. Routledge, London, England 1929 & Evans (2nd edition), 1949.

The Significance of Children's Play: Cass, Joan E.; Batsford Ltd., London, England, 1971.

BIBLIOGRAPHY: Special purpose books & articles

A.B.C. of Music: Holst, Imogen, Oxford University Press, Toronto, 1963.

Brain Research and Music: English W.; Paper C.M.E.A. Vancouver, B.C. 1979.

Harmony Fun with the Auto Harp: Krone, Neil A. Kijos Music Co. New York, 1967.

Implication of Brain Learning: D. Wilson paper I.S.M.E. Poland 1980.

Musical Ability in Children and its Measurement: Bentley, A. Harrap, G. London, England, 1966.

Method for Recorder, Book 1: Duschene, Mario, B.M.I. Berandol Music Ltd., Scarborough, Ontario, 1967.

Music for the Handicapped Child: Alvin, Juliette. Oxford University Press, Toronto, 1965.

Music Therapy: Alvin, Juliette, John Clare Books, London, England, 1966, 1975 and 1983.

The Foreign Language Innovation Curricula Study. Ann Arbor, Michigan, U.S.A. 1976.

The Many Ways to Play the Auto Harp: Schmidt, Oscar. International Inc., New Jersey, U.S.A. 1966.

The Slow Learner: Dobbs, J.P.B. Oxford University Press, London 1966.

The Wonderful World of Music: Britten, Benjamin and Holst, Imogen. Doubleday, New York, 1958.

The Tuning of the World: Schafer, Murray. McClelland & Stewart, Toronto, Ontario. 1977.

BIBLIOGRAPHY: The Arts

Council for Research in Music Education Bullet No. 57, 1977.

Reason and Emotion: John MacMurray, Faber and Faber, London, England, 1935.

The Arts in Schools: Calouste Gulberkian Foundation, Lisbon & London England, 1984.

APPENDIX IX
Discography

Beech, Sandra: *Chickery Chick,* (and cassette) Toronto, People Promotions Inc. PPI-001, 198?
Beech, Sandra: *Inch by Inch,* (and cassette) Toronto, Attic Records, 198?
Beech, Sandra: *Sunshine Songs,* (and cassette) Toronto Attic Records, 1982.
Baillargeon, Hélène, *Chez Hélène & More Chez Hélène,* Camden Records.
Bishop, Heather: *Belly Button,* Woodmore Manitoba, Mother of Pearl Records, 1982.
Brandywine: *Breakfast with Brandywine,* Edmonton, Pancake Records, 1981.
Butler, Rick (Compiler): *The Children's Collection* (Vol. 1), Scarborough, Tapestry, 1982.
Carfra, Pat: *Lullabies and Laughter,* (and cassette) Victoria, JQF Productions, 1982.
Carr, Rachel: *See and Be,* Caedmon Records T.C. 1684, 1981.
Cass-Beggs, Barbara and Michael: *Your Baby Needs Music* (Cassette), Ottawa, 1982.
Cooney, Michael: *Pure Unsweetened,* Toronto, Alliance Records, 1982.
Cruikshank, Ralph (Edited and selected by): *Canada's Favourite Folksongs for Kids,* Toronto, Berandol, BER 9031 1977.
Fowke, Edith (Compiler): *Sally Go Round the Sun,* Toronto McClelland and Stewart (RCA), T-56666 and T-56667, 1969.
Glazier, Tom: *Let's Sing Finger Plays,* (cassette) C.M.S. 688, 1977.
Guthrie, Woody: *Songs to Grow on, Book One,* Folkways, F.C. 7015.
Friendly Giant (Bob Homme): *The Giant Concert of Concerts,* Toronto, Kids' Records, KRL 1002 (CBC Merchandising, 1981).
Hann, Paul: *Brand New Boogaloo Zoo.* Edmonton, Mudpie Records, MUD 2 1982.
Jarrett, Merrick and Kathy: *Sing Along!* Toronto, Flutterby Records, 1981.
Jenkins, Ella: *Rhythms and Game Songs for the Little Ones.* F.C. 7680, 1964.
Jim and Rosalie: *At the Music Factory.* Toronto, Flutterby Records, 1981.
McGrath & Smithrim: *Baby Record,* (Cassette) Kid' Records, A.G.M. Records of Canada, Ltd. 1983.
Mike & Michelle: *Bunyips, Bunnies & Brumbies,* Elephant Records, Sydney, Australia, 1980.
Mills, Alan: *French Folk Songs for Children,* FC7017, Folkways Records.
English Folk Songs for Children, FC 7018, Folkways Records
Animals & More Animal Songs, FC 7018, Folkways Records
More Songs to Grown On, FC 7009, Folkways Records
MITS (Mariposa in the Schools): *Going Bananas.* Toronto, Mariposa Folk Foundation, 1979.
Mouskouri, Nana: *Pour les Enfants,* Fontana Records, 1967.
Murray, Anne: *There's a Hippo in My Bathtub.* Mississauga, Capitol, 1977.
Nagler, Eric: *Fiddle Up a Tune.* Toronto, Elephant Records, 1982.
Offenheim, Sandy: *If Snowflakes Fell in Flavours.* Toronto, Berandol, BER 9001. 197?
Paley, Lee and Sady: *Sing Me Sun.* Calgary, His Kids Records. HKR 823301 1982.

Penner, Fred: *The Cat Came Back*. Toronto, Troubadour Records, TR-009 1980.

Penner Fred: *The Polka Dot Pony*. Toronto, Troubadour. TR-0020 1981.

Pinel, Suzanne: *Un cadeau pour toi*. (and casette) Montréal, Productions Marc Ltée, MP 1047 197?

Pinel, Suzanne: *Une Giraffe à l'école,* (and cassette) 1982.

Pinel, Suzanne: *Je m'appelle Marie-soleil Bonjour!* (and cassette) 1982.

Pinel, Suzanne: *Comme Moi,* (and cassette) Marc Records MP 1084 1983.

Raffi: *The Corner Grocery Store*. Toronto, Troubadour Records. TR-007 1979.

Raffi: *Singable Songs for the Very Young*. Toronto, Elephant Records, TR-002 1976.

Raffi: *Rise and Shine*. Troubadour Records, TR-0023 1982.

Raffi: *More Singable Songs*. Toronto, Troubadour, TR-0010 1980.

Seeger, Pete: *Birds, Beasts, Bugs & Fishes*. Folkways Records, FC 7610, 1955.

Sharon, Lois and Bram: *One Elephant, Deux Elephants*. Toronto, Elephant Records, LFN 7801 1978.

Sharon, Lois and Bram: *Smorgasbord*. Toronto, Elephant Records, LFN 7902 1980.

Sharon, Lois and Bram: *Singing 'n Swinging*. Toronto, Elephant Records, LFN 8105 1981.

Sharon, Lois and Bram: *One. Two, Three, Four, Look Who's Coming through the Door*. Toronto, Elephant Records 1982.

Travellers: *Merry-Go-Round*. Toronto, Elephant records, LFN 8003 1980.

Valdy: *Valdy's Kid's Record*, Toronto, Sloth Records (dist: A & M Records) SLC 1003 198?

Walden, David and Birkenshaw, Lois (Producers): *The Goat With the Bright Red Socks*. Toronto, Berandol, BER 10011 1984.

Records for children's enjoyment which can also be used in their music classes:

Adventures in Music, R.C.A. Victor albums 1, 2 & 3.

Sound Records (clocks, bells, animals, etc.) EMI Records, Hayes, Middlesex, U.K.

APPENDIX X
A Selection of Canadian Musical Resources

BANFF: Can. Assoc. of Youth Orchestras, c/o Banff Scool of Fine Arts.

CALGARY: Canadian Folk Music Society (Mail order records) 1314 Sherbourne St. SW

EDMONTON: The Village Bookshop, (children's books & records) 10212 140 St., and **Audrey's** (Books) 10411 Jasper Ave.) and the **Universal Folklore Society** (music, referrals) 424-4653 **Academy of Country Music Entertainment,** 9312-150 Ave.

HALIFAX: Halifax Folklore Centre (music) 1528 Brunswick; Pair of Trindles (books) Historic properties, the waterfront; *Woozles* (children's books) 1533 Birmingham.

MONTREAL: Archambault Musique (music shop); **Jeunesses musicales du Canada**, 5253 ave. du Parc, suite 600; **CAMMAC**, Box 353, Westmount.

OTTAWA: The Bookery (children's books) 541 Sussex Drive; **Librairie Trillium** (French books) 281 Dalhousie; **Future Resources** (preschool music & equipment); 261 Richmond Road; **Ottawa-Carleton Summer Orchestra** 1683 Merivale.

QUEBEC CITY: La Procure générale, (books and mail order music) 600, côtes d'Abraham; **Contact musique** (music books) 578 rue St-Jean.

REGINA: Don Hatton's (music shop) 7057 Hamilton; **Children's Corner**, (children's books & records) 2335 11th Avenue.

ST. CATHARINE'S: Canadian Music Educator' Assoc. 34 Cameron Rd.

TORONTO: Children's Bookstore (children's books & records) Mirvish Village, 604 Markham St. M6G 2L8; **Louise Kool & Son** (preschool music & equipment) 1147 Bellamy, Scarborough; **Remenyi's,** (music shop) 210 Bloor Street; **Interprovincial Music Camps,** 821 Eglington Ave., W.

VANCOUVER: Ward (music) 412 West Hastings; **Duthie's Books** 1751 W. 2nd Ave.; **Teacher's Store** (educational toys, games, books) 2031 South, Park Royal. Empire Music 8553 Main St.

WINNIPEG: Growing Minds (children's books) 269 Edmonton St.; **Long & McQuade** (music shop) 755 Corydon; **Mary Score** (books) Grahame Avenue.

WOODSTOCK: Canadian Music Therapy Assoc., Box 1208, Ontario, N4S 8T6.

Canadian Cataloguing in Publication Data

Cass-Beggs, Barbara, 1904-
    Your child needs music

Bibliography: p.
Includes index.
ISBN 0-88797-268-3

1. Music - Instruction and study - Juvenile.
2. Music in the home. I. Title.

ML83.C38 1986   780'.7   C86-094186-8

CREDITS:

The author would like to thank the following for material used in the LISTEN-LIKE-LEARN programme.

For Day's Work and Week's Work, Collected by Marjorie Kennedy-Fraser. Words A.M. Mackenzie Air M. Macleod. Boosey & Hawkes Vol. 3, 1921.
I's the By that Builds the Boat, Folk, Newfoundland, Folk Songs of Canada, Fowke & Johnston, Waterloo Music Co. Ltd. Ontario, 1954.
Jack In a Box, Louie E. de Rusette, 1929.
Johnny Writes, Collected by Ms. Cynthia Raza from Gallion's Mount Primary School, London, England, 1975.
Land of the Silver Birch, Folk, Canadian Collected Merrick Jarrett. Included in "Folk Songs of Canada", Fowke & Johnston Waterloo Music Co. Ltd. Ontario, 1954.
Ah! Si Mon Moine Voulait Danser! Folk, French Canadian. Gagnon, Barbeau, Gibbon & Fowke. Included in "Folk Songs of Canada" Waterloo Music Co. Ltd. 1954.
When I 'tink of nice girl Liza Folk Jamaican, Collected by Thomas Wood, Oxford University Press, 1927.
Donkey Riding Folk Canadian, Colcord, Doerflighter, Flowke. Included in "Folk Songs of Canada", Waterloo Music Co. Ltd. Ontario, 1954.
Who Has Seen the Wind, Folk Spanish, words: Christine Rosetti. Included in "Sound Beginnings" Slind, Churchley & Haines, McGraw Hill Co. 1967.
Up the Ladder We Will Go, Diller & Page, G. Schirmer Inc. 1936.
The Baby Goes to Boston, Laura E. Richards, from "Tirra-lirra", Little, Brown & Co.

The following have been used with permission:
"Mix a Pancake" from **This Little Puffin**, Elizabeth Matterson, Penguin Books, Ltd., London, England.
"Orders" *A.M. Klein*, **The Wind Has Wings**, Oxford University Press, 1968.
"Happiness" *A.A. Milne*, **When We Were Very Young**, 1924.
"Walk, Walk, softly slow" *D. Amundson & McDonald*, **Learning Time with Language Experience for Young Children**, McGraw-Hill, 1968.
"The Baby Goes to Boston", *Laura E. Richards*.
"Here is a tree with its leaves so green", Pitman Ltd., England.
"Fingers like to wiggle-waggle", Novello & Co., England
"Here is a beehive", *Emile Poulson*, J. Curwen & Sons Ltd., England.
"Ten Galloping Horses", *Mrs. Wyn Daniel Evans*, England.
"Tiger walking through the night", **All Sorts of Everything** *M. Garrick, ed.,* W. Heinemann Ltd.

Except as noted, songs and poems used herein are in the public domain and may be used by readers without permission. The author would like to thank the
Day Nurseries Branch, Dept. of Social & Family Services, c/o Queen's Park, Toronto, Ontario, and **The Association for Early Childhood Education, Ottawa Branch** for being sources of many of these songs and poems.

NOTE: The author and publisher have made every effort to credit and trace songs and poems used in this book. Any oversight should be brought to the attention of the publisher in order to correct future editions.

Thanks go to the **Canadian Folk Music Society** for the use of their record list.

Photography by Lorna Cheriton and Linda Carrier-Walker.
Illustrations by Simon Baumberg   Design and editing: W. G. Cheriton.